Accommodation and Social Cohesion in the Urban Environment — the Implications for Young People

The School for Advanced Urban Studies at the University of Bristol is an international centre for research, teaching and consultancy. Concerned primarily with the analysis and development of public policy, it works increasingly with international policy organisations while retaining a commitment to support locally-based initiatives. Enquiries about any aspect of the School's work may be made via the authors of this booklet, or the School's publicity officer, Carroll Pierce, at the address below.

**School for Advanced Urban Studies
Rodney Lodge
Grange Road
Bristol BS84EA
UK**

Accommodation and Social Cohesion in the Urban Environment — the Implications for Young People

Paul Burton, Ray Forrest, Murray Stewart,
School for Advanced Urban Studies
University of Bristol, UK

CONSOLIDATED REPORT
January 1989

ACCOMMODATION AND SOCIAL COHESION IN THE URBAN ENVIRONMENT — THE IMPLICATIONS FOR YOUNG PEOPLE

This publication is also available in the following languages:

FR — ISBN 92-826-0021-1
ES — ISBN 92-826-0019-x

Cataloguing data can be found at the end of this publication.

Luxembourg: Office for Official Publications of European Communities

ISBN: 92-826-0020-3
Catalogue number: SY-56-89-287-EN-C

© Copyright: THE EUROPEAN FOUNDATION FOR THE IMPROVEMENT OF LIVING AND WORKING CONDITIONS, 1989. For rights of translation or reproduction, applications should be made to the Director, European Foundation for the Improvement of Living and Working Conditions, Loughlinstown House, Shankill, County Dublin, Ireland.

Printed in Ireland

The European Foundation for the Improvement of Living and Working Conditions

CONTENTS

		Page
1.	Introduction	1
2.	Key Themes and Issues	5
	* Structural change and unemployment	5
	* Marginality and exclusion	6
	* Young people	7
	- growing up and leaving home	8
	- marginality and social cohesion	9
	- discrimination	10
	- homelessness and rooflessness	11
	- transferability of interventions and responses	12
3.	Young People: Family, Employment and Accommodation	13
	- the position of young people in Europe	13
	- leaving the family home	20
	- young people in the labour market	25
	- housing opportunities for young people	34
4.	Responses to the Housing Problems Faced by Young People	43
	- Italy	44
	- France	49
	- The Netherlands	55
	- Federal Republic of Germany	63
	- England	68
	- Ireland	72
	- Greece	74
	- Portugal	76
	- Spain	77
5.	Comparisons, Conclusions and Recommendations	81
	- background	81
	- comparisons	84
	- conclusions and prognosis	91
	- main findings	92
	- recommendations	97

ACKNOWLEDGEMENTS

This report is a synthesis of the work carried out in 1987 by nine different research groups in different countries of Europe. The separate reports of the nine teams amounted in aggregate to some 750 pages; all of the reports are tightly argued and heavily illustrated with statistics, analyses and examples of initiatives. It is impossible to reflect this volume of work in a single synthesis and we have therefore drawn selectively from the various studies.

We would, however, wish to acknowledge our debt to Peter Jablonka, Philip Potter and Lutz Unterseher (SALSS, Federal Republic of Germany); Gerard Bauer and Gerard Cuzon (CODRA, France); Maurizio Di Palma and Massimo Pazienti (ECOTER, Italy); Tjeerd Deelstra and Jaap Schokkenbroek (Netherlands); Ximena George-Nascimento (Spain); Dimitris Emmanuel (Greece); Tom Ronayne (Irish Foundation for Human Development, Ireland); Clara Mendes and Luis Carneiro (Portugal).

We would also wish to thank our research manager, Wendy O'Conghaile for her assistance in the assembly of the material and for her guidance in its progress towards a coherent final form.

Last but by no means least we must record our gratitude to the Research Secretaries for coping so admirably with our handwriting, alterations and deadlines in typing this report.

Preface

As its first major item of work on living conditions, the Foundation commissioned at the end of 1984 a review entitled "Living Conditions in Urban Areas". This report examined the ways in which current social and economic changes were affecting the quality of life experienced by different population groups in different parts of European cities. Urban society was seen to be increasingly polarised and geographically segregated. Disadvantaged groups such as the unemployed, single-parent families, migrant workers and the elderly tended to be living in poorer environments in the inner cities and on the urban fringe. This increased marginalisation and segregation was clearly brought out through an analysis of research and policy on questions of population change, the role of the family, economic restructuring, the provision of housing, citizen participation and the role of the voluntary sector.

As well as providing the Foundation with a state-of-the-art picture of urban living conditions, the review was also to enable the Foundation to determine the scope and content of its 1985-88 programme on the urban environment. One of the main items of this programme concerned the situation of underprivileged groups, particularily in relation to accommodation and physical and social environment. The elderly and long-term unemployed were already subjects of specific research programmes. Young people, although a significant focus in other European Community programmes, had not at that time been taken account of in Foundation work. The review, however, consistently pointed to the way in which changes in work and employment structure were negatively impacting on many young Europeans. While these work impacts were the focus of considerable European level attention, little attention had been paid to the effects of their employment difficulties on their ability to obtain satisfactory accommodation and good living conditions or of the effects of poor living conditions on opportunities to find work or avail of training.

Young people are at the entry point to both labour and housing markets as they make the transition to adulthood. Traditionally work has provided the income, status and often the "training" for becoming an accepted adult member of society, eventually leading to the establishment of a new and separate household. With so many young people experiencing extended periods of unemployment and/or low income, this time of passage was inevitably becoming more difficult and putting larger numbers at risk of longer term disadvantage and deprivation, with severe implications for the future of urban society. Indeed increasing attention was being drawn to some of the danger signals — increasing drug and alcohol abuse, vandalism and petty crime, hooliganism and other deviant behaviour.

It was in this context that the Foundation requested a multi-disciplinary team of researchers to assess the situation facing young people in the Community, focussing on issues of housing and social/family circumstances. The team was also asked to highlight existing policies and practical experiences aimed at improving the living conditions of young people and to define policy issues which could be the focus of future action.

This consolidated report brings together the main findings of the five main national studies and four shorter reviews undertaken between 1987 and 1988. It examines the relationships between the changes taking place in housing and labour markets and the way in which they are affecting the life chances of different groups of young Europeans. The evidence, gathered primarily from existing sources, indicates that a small but growing minority of young people are suffering exclusion and marginalisation and that this is often inextricabily bound up with their lack of access to suitable accommodation. Changes in the structure and amount of available work, the varying role and capacity of family to provide support, the rigidities of housing policy and provision are combining to create situations of real crisis for some groups of young people and there appears to be little recognition of their problems. Most responses highlighted by the research team were small scale and often developed solely by the voluntary sector. On the positive side this work, however, points to the capacity and willingness of young people to participate in elaborating and implementing solutions to their problems if given the necessary support.

In December 1988 a meeting was held in Brussels to enable representatives of the employers, trade unions, governments and the Commission of the European Communities — the constituent bodies of the Foundation's Administrative Board — to evaluate the findings of this research. The participants stressed the value of this new area of research, which should be viewed in the whole context of urban and regional change and the development of the internal market. Questions of availability and access to suitable and affordable housing become even more significant in the context of increasing labour mobility. It is necessary, however, to take account of all the aspects of the multiple difficulties facing the most disadvantaged young people in our cities. This report, it was felt, would help policy-makers better understand the range of problems and how they sometimes interacted to create situations of real crisis.

However, in conclusion the representatives agreed that this consolidated report, which should be studied in conjunction with the more detailed national reports, could only form a starting point for dealing with young people's situation in a more comprehensive way. The research did nevertheless provide valuable data to inform the debate which should follow this work. After agreeing some minor amendments, the evaluation Committee approved the publication of this report.

Wendy O'Conghaile
Research Manager
European Foundation for the Improvement of
Living and Working Conditions
Dublin, July 1989

CHAPTER 1: INTRODUCTION

The European Commission has often stressed the importance of young people as the European citizens of tomorrow and has continuously expressed its concern at the gravity of the situation for a growing number of young people. A whole range of policy proposals have been made in this respect and have been reflected in a series of Council Resolutions on employment, education and training. However, young people still bear a disproportionate burden of unemployment and of instability of employment and this is inevitably having severe effects in other areas of their lives. A growing proportion of young people lack a clear place within society and continuing deprivation of non-work life can make finding a job and developing a working career all the more impossible. There is already considerable concern over problems of homelessness, drug and alcohol abuse and crime and vandalism amongst young people, whilst labour market and education/training measures and the development of special schemes and projects to assist the young unemployed are crucial policy elements in the solution of these problems. The roles of good and stable accommodation and of satisfactory family and social life are also vital but have tended to receive less attention in the European context.

This report extends the contribution of the Foundation to a more integrated approach which takes account of economic, social and environmental factors. It addresses issues of the urban environment, accommodation, and social cohesion through an analysis of the living conditions of young people in disadvantaged urban areas. Particular attention is paid to accommodation, and to family and social life. This research has built upon the earlier work of the Foundation (Living Conditions in Urban Europe) which argued that disparities in living conditions are likely to continue and to become more pronounced. Observable processes of differentiation, segregation and marginalisation will reinforce these disparities for particular groups. These social tendencies are reflected very differently in different countries, cities and neighbourhoods however, and the Foundation thus commissioned a multi-national research project to extend the arguments developed both in its 'living conditions' study and in a set of related research initiatives on urban services, the long-term unemployed and the role of the voluntary sector. The objectives of this major research study were:

- to provide information on the accommodation and family/social situation of young people (approximately 18-25 years) in urban areas to policy-makers at national and European level;

- to highlight existing policies and practical experiences in a number of member States aimed at improving the living conditions of such young people in relation to accommodation and family/social environment;

- through a cross-national exchange of information and experience, to define policy issues and areas in this context which could be the subject of Community action to improve the situation of young people in urban areas.

These objectives were pursued through a linked set of nationally-based studies and this report is thus in practice a synthesis of nine separate research studies. In France, Germany, Italy and the Netherlands major national cross-studies were carried out involving first a description and an analysis at the national level of the social and economic position of young people; secondly a description of relevant policies and programmes relating to young people, welfare systems, accommodation, family and so on; and thirdly studies of specific localities aiming to identify the specific regional and urban context within which the accommodation problems of young people are set and the existence or otherwise of local responses to the needs of young people.

The four national studies were complemented by a further smaller study of England and by shorter reviews of Greece, Ireland, Portugal and Spain. The project brief recognised of course that variations would exist between countries in terms of the problems facing young people, the causes of these problems and the types of initiative developed in response. The brief also emphasised, however, that significant differences might exist within countries, for example between richer and poorer areas, urban and rural settings, inner and outer parts of cities, and large cities and smaller towns. These considerations led to the selection of two 'local' case studies within each of the four main countries studied and in England, and in the shorter reviews the Spanish (Barcelona) and Irish (Dublin) reviews in effect also amounted to local case studies.

Whilst the separate national studies all worked to a common brief, were asked to address the same key themes, and prepared their reports to a common format, there was no attempt to impose an artificial framework or to suppress the richness or specificity which emerged from the national studies. Thus whilst the themes and issues are common to all national case-studies (see Chapter 2 below) the particular features of the case-studies are in a sense free-standing. Their conclusions are justified and meaningful on the one hand in the contexts of the particular economic, social and cultural parameters of individual countries, and on the other hand in the context of a European-wide analysis of some aspects of the employment and accommodation experience of young people.

The structure and content of this report attempts to reflect both these elements - the general and common features of young people's accommodation problems across the range of Community countries and at the same time the specificity of the circumstances of young people's living conditions in the particular localities studied.

Chapter 2 looks particularly to the common themes and issues. Building upon the earlier 'Living Conditions' research it establishes five main elements to which subsequent chapters return. These elements or themes are, first, growing up and leaving home, second, marginality and social cohesion, third, discrimination, fourth, homelessness and rooflessness, and fifth, the transferability of intervention and response. Chapter 3 offers a predominantly analytical synthesis of the assumptions and conceptions about young people contained in the various national studies. The chapter takes three main strands of young people's experience - the relationship to the family, the relationship to work and the relationship to accommodation and rehearses the interdependence of these relationships as they affect young people's living conditions.

Chapter 4 by contrast offers a more descriptive view of the nine national studies, and in an attempt to do justice to the richness of the research material briefly summarises both the various and varied responses to young people's housing needs evident in the different countries and the sub-national locality studies of particular regions or cities. Chapter 5 rehearses some of the main arguments for looking at young people and then presents our main findings on a comparative basis. It then draws conclusions about the major trends affecting young people's opportunities and, finally, presents a series of recommendations directed at policy makers, practitioners and other researchers.

CHAPTER 2: KEY THEMES AND ISSUES

Structural Change and Unemployment

Over the last two decades, European Community countries have experienced marked economic, social and demographic changes. In many countries it was the early 1970s which saw the beginning of a period of recession and fiscal retrenchment. In others, the impact of economic restructuring and global recession came earlier or later. It is not possible to draw firm chronological boundaries around a particular phase of economic and social change, nor is it sensible to imply that the previous period was characterised by stability. Social and economic transformations vary in their impact intra and inter nationally and the seeds of those transformations are found in the transformations of previous periods. One of the valuable contributions of cross-national research however is to demonstrate that apparently minor shifts in the socio-economic structure, or the social policy of one country form part of a more significant process affecting a number of countries in different ways.

The end of the long post-war boom in the late 1960s and early 1970s occasioned a number of interrelated changes. The old industrial centres rapidly lost investment and employment. Unemployment in those areas and sectors rose rapidly. There was increased competition from countries such as Japan and the newly industrialised nations. High inflation rates and dwindling productivity produced severe public expenditure pressures, evident at both local and national level. The structures of welfare states which had been established in the post-war period came under increasing fiscal and ideological pressure. New political regimes emerged with programmes of deregulation and privatisation which represented a sharp rupture from the consensus politics of the post-war era. And across the political spectrum there was evident disillusionment with old prescriptions for social problems and social inequalities which involved direct intervention by large scale state bureaucracies. Increasingly, the emphasis was on government as the enabler of privatised alternatives, on self-help, self-reliance and on smaller scale, more responsive forms of intervention.

The nature and location of employment has also begun to change although it would be wrong to exaggerate the scale and pace of those developments. Nevertheless, the more obvious impacts of economic restructuring such as rising unemployment and broad sectoral shifts from manufacturing to service employment conceal more complex and subtle developments affecting the scale and nature of industrial and commercial enterprises, where they are located and who they recruit and retain. Typically these developments are described in terms of greater flexibility. A new generation of productive enterprises employs new technology to facilitate more rapid changes in what is provided and how it is produced. This is contrasted with the large scale and rather rigid nature of mass production.

Marginality and Exclusion

There are, and have been, inevitable human casualties as these changes have occurred. Such casualties have been variously referred to as 'the excluded', 'the new underclass', marginal or peripheral. Poverty is not the sole or even the necessary condition of marginality encompassing as it does the processes of helplessness, oppression, underprivilege, non-participation and state dependence. Different groups are peripheral and excluded in different ways. And it is a relative concept referring to a continuum of participation and non-participation, inclusion or exclusion. It is also relative in the sense that the nature of that continuum will vary nationally and culturally.

Some commentators suggest that the symbiotic relationship between mass production and mass consumption which produced (or at least promised) a pervasive, inclusive social consumption norm, buttressed by an expanding welfare state, is giving way to a more competitive, individualistic and differentiated pattern of social and economic participation. State expenditure may become more oriented towards directly productive investment, increasingly concerned with rewards and subsidies for individuals rather than groups and there will be mounting economic, political and ideological pressure to constrain and control the various forms of income support and transfer payments. For those competing in the formal labour market there is likely to be greater volatility, uncertainty and a more differentiated income and reward structure. In those countries where welfare mechanisms have become established and significant features of the post-war era, the reorientation and restructuring of the welfare state, will lead to a re-emphasis on family support, family resources and social networks in the shaping of life chances. And within this broad scenario a common theme is one of <u>exclusion</u> or <u>marginality</u> for those unable to compete effectively within a more privatised social and economic environment. This <u>marginalisation or exclusion is multi-dimensional encompassing homelessness, unemployment, insecure and low paid employment, isolation and loneliness, discrimination and stigmatisation</u>. Moreover these <u>processes are interconnected</u>, hence the importance emphasised in the overview report which preceded this study of an understanding of economic restructuring to the development of thinking on housing and living conditions. It must also be recognised that marginality can take many different forms referring as it does to a myriad of disparate groups. Whilst exclusion may be a common experience among a growing minority it would be quite wrong to assume that the nature and consequences of that exclusion are the same for groups as different as inner city ethnic minorities, single parents on peripheral estates, low paid agricultural workers, frail and impoverished elderly people and so on. Any assessment of the consequences of recent social and economic change must be sensitive to aspects of gender, race, class and, indeed, the life cycle.

Young People

It is against this kind of background that young people emerged as a group which required more detailed study. The overview (see Chapter 1) report argued that an examination of living conditions in urban areas should be pursued along three simple dimensions: a <u>socio-economic dimension</u> (principally in relation to position in the labour and housing markets); a <u>spatial dimension</u> (where people live in regions, cities or neighbourhoods); <u>life cycle stage</u> (family and household circumstances).

Rising unemployment and the changing pattern of housing opportunities have had a disproportionate impact on young people. Moreover, 'youth' has emerged as a particular focus of discussion of policy at both national and European levels. For research which seeks to combine an understanding of both the dynamics of the labour and housing markets, young people were an obvious focus. The transition from school to work or higher education, from the parental home to independent living, from dependence to full citizenship, from single status to marriage or cohabitation are often intimately connected. The nature of those relationships, the closeness of the connections, the sequence and timing will, however, vary between countries, between different groups of young people and may well have a spatial dimension. One of the primary aims of this report is to go beyond rather general and bland statements about differentiation and marginality and emphasise that not only do the majority of young people negotiate the key transitional stages relatively unproblematically (indeed, there are some groups of young people who are experiencing increasing affluence) but that patterns and processes of disadvantage must be grounded in specific social, spatial and cultural milieux. To be a young, unemployed, white male living on a council estate in the north of England will be a quite different experience from being, say, a young female Surinamese single parent on a peripheral estate in the Netherlands. And an understanding of these kinds of contrasts and of the different institutional structures in different countries leads to a more sensitive understanding of varying governmental and non-governmental responses to issues of young homelessness or youth unemployment.

Many of the issues discussed above will be elaborated in later sections of this report. It is appropriate at this stage to provide a brief summary of the main themes and issues addressed. These fall under four main headings.

(a)   Growing up and leaving the family home

What are the typical patterns and pathways? To what extent are there defined and contrasting routes for young women as opposed to young men? Is the family home becoming a longer term refuge for the young? How do factors such as educational participation, income support policies, the differential impact of employment and underemployment, military service, housing costs and availability, different attitudes and expectations combine to constrain certain groups of young people? What are the significant variations cross-nationally?

A discussion of these issues goes beyond a consideration of structural changes in the labour and housing markets nationally and cross-nationally and takes us into a complex literature concerned with the sociology of family life. There are important cultural and class variations involved both within and between countries and we can only touch upon some of the more important aspects in a report of this length and in a research project of this breadth. It is clear, however, that we have to take account of the broader dynamics of the household and not see the young person (or people) in isolation from the other members of the family. For example, the young adult son or daughter may earn an important component of the overall household income, and this may act as a constraint on their mobility. Family size, parental earnings and occupation, the size, quality and location of the family home will all affect patterns of departure by young people. Different groups of young people may stay longer in the family home for quite different reasons.

(b)   **Marginality and social cohesion**

The issues here revolve around participation in the social and cultural norms of the majority and the extent to which non-participation is governed by constraint rather than choice. It would be erroneous for example to confuse marginality, deviancy and non-conformity. Again this is a complex area where social pathology models of deviancy among young people blurs into structural models of exclusion. Moreover, we must consider how far the present circumstances of disadvantage and deviancy among groups of young people is part of a longer term trajectory. Will the next generation of entrants to the housing and labour market face quite different circumstances and have quite different experiences? In other words, are there segments of young people drifting away into a marginal and uncertain future, disillusioned with, and despairing of, the conventional routes to social, economic and political participation. This may be particularly true of the young long-term unemployed and never employed. It is this group who have not been habituated into the work process, who have not experienced the social discipline of regular employment. Limited state support through welfare payments or training schemes tends to deny them access to the consumption standards of the majority of young people. Non-participation in the formal labour market denies them access to work based forms of political and social participation such as trades unions although some trades unions have active youth sections and organise, among other things, political education programmes. Statistically they are likely to be part of a marginalised household and a disproportionate number will be from the ethnic minorities and/or the less privileged sections of the working class.

There are fears that the social cement is crumbling at the edges and that these processes of marginality may have dangerous and destructive consequences for the social fabric as a whole. Indeed, part of the background and motivation for research in this area is the need to find alternative forms of inclusion for young people who are bombarded with ever proliferating needs and aspirations, yet have deteriorating means of fulfilling them. It would of course be foolish to believe that formal employment in any shape or form is all that is required. There are issues of job satisfaction and dignity which go beyond that. Nevertheless, if the labour market can no longer function as it once did then satisfactory alternatives must be found otherwise governments may be faced with greater deviancy and disruption and be forced into more overt forms of social control.

The role of the family has a prominent place in current discussions of social cohesion. Whilst the extended family continues to be dominant in many parts of southern Europe, in countries such as the UK, the Netherlands and the Federal Republic of Germany, the trend towards smaller households and early household formation is well established. There are enormous cultural differences in the social and economic role of the family in different countries. And the relationship between the family and social cohesion are somewhat complex and confused. In countries with a long history of welfare intervention, family values and family care are being re-asserted as the alternative to insensitive and profligate state agencies. Equally, however, few commentators have suggested that young people should stay at home longer. Indeed, it is assumed implicitly at least that 'the "problem" is delayed' and frustrated departure from the family home breeds destructive and deviant attitudes which tend to hinder development to adulthood and full citizenship. In countries with less developed welfare states and where children typically stay at home well into their twenties the situation is quite different. Moreover, the apparently positive attitudes of many young people towards living with their family is difficult to disentangle from the recognition that there are few economically viable alternatives.

(c)   Discrimination

Another theme that runs through the report is the likelihood of increased discrimination as competition for housing and employment opportunities becomes more intense. This discrimination may take many forms ranging from overt racist attitudes and behaviour to more complex combinations of factors which produce discriminatory outcomes. In some countries, for example the Federal Republic of Germany, ethnic minorities are usually also classified as foreigners and suffer institutionalised discrimination as well as social exclusion. It may affect those who are disabled or mentally handicapped, working class women and single parent families. It may involve the negative labelling of young people who live in particular areas, say on a peripheral public housing estate. The consequences of suffering discrimination may produce further discrimination as being young and never employed becomes itself a stigmatising factor. Where access to adequate housing requires a satisfactory credit rating or where there is intense competition for rental housing among young people, those who face greatest difficulties will be those who may be regarded as high risk borrowers or as less desirable tenants, for example, young mothers with children and members of black and other ethnic minorities.

(d) Homelessness and rooflessness

There has been an evident increase in homelessness in general and among young people in particular. As is made clear later in the report there are great definitional differences among countries regarding homelessness. Whereas in the UK the definition of homelessness has an official and legislative dimension this is not so in most European countries. Indeed it is not a particularly meaningful statistic in many contexts, for example, where there is easy access to cheap, low quality accommodation. Hence there is a need to distinguish between being without shelter and being homeless. Being without a secure and stable home environment is much more widespread and even more difficult to measure. Moreover, different groups of young people may become homeless, and respond to that experience in different ways.

The rising numbers of young people who seem to be living on the margins of society in insecure and unsatisfactory accommodation is one dimension of more controversial claims regarding the re-emergence of mass poverty and growing social polarisation. The term 'new homeless' is commonly used to denote a rather different set of circumstances from those which prevailed in many countries in previous decades. Again, it refers to a view that progressive <u>inclusion</u> (eg the spread of good quality housing, secure jobs) has given way to <u>exclusion</u> and the divergence of the majority from the minority. It is the parallel development of deprivation and decay with rampant and burgeoning affluence. Inner urban areas are gentrified and exclusive waterside residences and hi-tech business parks co-exist with hostels for the homeless and displaced. As is commented later, it is often those areas which have served as the traditional 'survival' areas for low income young people which are subject to greatest change.

(e) The transferability of interventions and responses

The justification for comparative or cross-national policy research lies in part in its potential for offering insights into the social scientific explanation of economic and social phenomena in different countries and in part in its capacity to generate practical innovations in one country which draw upon the experience of their application elsewhere. On the one hand there is the search for a European commonality analysis, explanation and prescription and on the other hand there is the capacity to explain variation, specificity and differentiation between countries and regions and to borrow and experiment with interventions drawn from different and contrasting settings. Cross-national research has the virtue of challenging established notions of appropriate policy responses; indeed one of the main justifications for comparative analysis is this 'shock value'. At the same time there are examples of the over simple transfer of ideas or practices from one national situation to another without sufficient reference to the conditions under which such a transfer can succeed. Just as in medical science transplants can be rejected by recipient body, so in social science can socio-economic policy interventions be implanted into an unwelcoming and unreceptive context. The notion of transferability of experience therefore is one which lies at the heart of the practical relevance and application of the Foundation's research.

CHAPTER 3: YOUNG PEOPLE: FAMILY, EMPLOYMENT AND ACCOMMODATION

In this section of the report we provide a general discussion of the issues facing young people in relation to the family, employment and accommodation. The research as a whole has focused on the experiences of young people in urban and urbanising areas in different countries. There is thus little specific discussion of the rural dimension although any strict separation of these spheres would be artificial and conceptually untenable. Nevertheless, it is in cities, however defined and conceptualised, that we find the large concentrations of young people, where we find the most marked patterns of differentiation and segregation and where young people face particular problems in negotiating complex social structures. For the majority of young people in Europe it is the urban experience which is pre-eminent in the shaping of their early employment and housing histories. It is in the urban domain where the majority of young people establish their independent identities, set up their own households and succeed or fail in realising their ambitions and aspirations.

The position of young people in Europe

At the outset it should be emphasised that young people are not, any more than say, elderly people, an undifferentiated mass who share common experiences and face common problems. The divisions which fragment and differentiate populations in general, most notably gender, class and race, are relevant to consideration of any stage in the (family) life cycle. It is simply inappropriate therefore to refer to the 'employment problems of young people' or the 'housing problems of elderly people' as if such broad categories in any sense share common problems. Once we move beyond national boundaries, these difficulties are compounded and the distinctions multiply according to specific patterns of economic development, different demographic trends, political and policy variations and specific cultural factors. Getting lost in the fine detail can of course induce analytic paralysis. In attempting to avoid superficiality and unwarranted generalisation, cross national studies can degenerate into a morass of distinctions and cautionary remarks.

In recognising and acknowledging that important differences exist, socially and spatially, we can nevertheless draw out some commonality in the experiences of young people and in the backcloth of social and economic change against which those experiences have occurred. There are particular features of the experiences of young people which occur regardless of class, culture or location. There are particular periods of transition, or rites of passage. There is the transition from education to work: from the family home to independent living: from child status to full citizenship: from transient and formative relationships to more robust, adult relationships. The majority of young people negotiate and experience these processes, albeit in different ways, and at different times. They are the particularities of that stage of the family life cycle. In this context Emmanuel refers to the project of forming a new household, a project which in the Greek context is linked inextricably with marriage and family (p 1). Similarly, Ronayne refers to the needs which emerge in relation to "....a range of normative transitions arising in the lives of young people as they move from adolescence to adult life" (p 3). The coincidence between these different transitions, for example school to work or family home to autonomous dwelling, varies among different countries and will be more or less problematic for different groups of young people. Di Palma et al point usefully to differentiated 'modes of participation in community life' among young people which may distinguish those dependent on state welfare policies and benefits from others better able to compete and survive in the mainstream of society. Such a conception points towards a consideration of marginality among young people and widely expressed fears that within the young urban population is an expanding, excluded, underclass who have borne the brunt of the far-reaching economic and social changes which have occurred in recent years. In this context a UNESCO report claimed that for young people in the 1980s, key words in their experiences were likely to be "....'scarcity', 'unemployment', 'underemployment', 'ill-employment', 'anxiety', 'defensiveness', 'pragmatism', and even 'subsistence' and 'survival' itself" (UNESCO, 1981, quoted in Ronayne). As we approach the 1990s such a dramatic characterisation may require some qualification and recognition that the experiences of young people in the labour and housing markets have become increasingly polarised rather than universally marginalised. This theme will, however, be pursued and elaborated in later sections.

It is possible at this stage to point to a number of broad structural changes which have had particular impact on young people. Arguably, these processes are evident in all the countries under consideration in this study although their significance and their consequences are inevitably varied. Throughout the 1980s all countries have experienced the effects of global economic recession and restructuring. One of the most notable impacts has been rapidly rising unemployment, certainly into the mid 1980s. Young people have been particularly vulnerable to increased competition in the job market and have suffered disproportionately as regards the incidence of unemployment. One consequence of this increasingly competitive job market has been creeping credentialism or 'qualification inflation' (Ronayne) among young people. To compete effectively in the formal labour market requires ever more paper qualifications. This prolongation of the educational period has a number of effects. It extends the period of dependency on parental incomes and, in many cases, the parental homes. It extends the period of low income for many young people and thus reduces their ability to achieve independence in the housing market. It also of course relieves, or at least delays, pressure on the labour market by involving greater numbers of young people in education often well into their twenties. In many ways, therefore, and contrary to popular belief, the family as a support system has regained its importance (although of course the extent to which it was ever eroded varies cross nationally).

This reduced effective demand among young people in the early stages of their housing and employment histories has therefore been the product of a number of processes (insecure or non-employment; longer periods in education; downward pressure on incomes in junior grades). It has, however, coincided with general fiscal retrenchment with pervasive cuts and reorientations in various forms of state benefits, subsidies and direct forms of state provision. For a number of reasons, some fiscal, some ideological, there has been a shift away from state towards market solutions. Reduced public investment has been most notable in housing provision, with a decline in the role of social housing. At the same time, most countries have continued to experience a fall in the availability of private sector lettings. This squeeze on the rental sector has hit young people particularly severely given their general dependence on this form of accommodation. Conversely, most governments have focused their fiscal and policy energies on the promotion of home ownership. Home ownership is, however, often an inappropriate form of housing tenure for those seeking easy access and easy mobility in the housing market. Moreover, in most countries it is well beyond the means of the average young person. At the same time, the fiscal squeeze has hit hardest at those regarded as being in low priority need. Young single people typically fall into this category while young couples with dependent children in some cases benefit from targeted policies.

Economic restructuring has also been reflected in the reshaping of the urban environment. Many cities have experienced a rapid gentrification of their old, industrial and dockland areas with a consequent loss of cheap, low quality, older properties which are typically the domain of students and other young people on marginal incomes. Bauer and Cuzon in their discussion of France, point to the "gradual disappearance of furnished digs ('hotels meubles') ... which have traditionally housed young people with insecure incomes during their transition between the family home and an independent adult status" (p 50). In the same vein, Jablonka et al comment on the "well-off households [who] have been moving back again to the old inner-city residential districts" and to the consequent displacement of low income households which is occurring in many German cities (p 33). And in relation to the Netherlands, and particularly Amsterdam, Deelstra and Schokkenbroek indicate the gentrifying pressures on the older parts of cities where young people are concentrated:

> Better-off, young to middle-aged, one and two-person households with no children (yuppies, dinkies and the like) have begun to concentrate in the urban centres. This group needs easy access at all times to shops, a wide range of service firms and such 'elitist cosmopolitan facilities' as theatres, museums, cinemas and cafes, which are largely concentrated in the city centre. (p 44)

Interestingly, they observe that those affluent groups among the young and middle-aged, by competing for inner urban residential locations with the more traditional users of that space (students, low income young people, young singles) may ultimately displace those groups to residential areas which are simply inappropriate for their lifestyles in terms of both transport facilities and dwelling form:

> A suburban environment intended almost exclusively for living - large single family dwellings with gardens in quiet, spacious, safe surroundings - is best suited to the way of life of the traditional family unit. (p 46)

This potential mismatch between dwelling form and the needs of young people is a theme common to many commentaries on national housing markets.

Demographic changes, new patterns of household fission and fusion associated with later marriage, divorce and remarriage, the general tendency towards more smaller and single person households, are placing new demands on housing stocks designed to cater for more conventional family structures. Moreover, national housing policies tend to be rather blind to the needs of non-family units. In the private sector this often reflects the lack of effective demand among certain groups, notably young single people. Within the public sector young, single people typically have low priority unless supply side factors (eg high vacancy rates) dictate more flexible allocation criteria (eg as in the Netherlands, some parts of the UK and some peripheral estates in cities in northern Germany).

The overall picture of developments in relation to labour and housing markets in the later 1970s and 1980s is one of sharp disruption, of systems slowly adjusting to new pressures and new demands. Traditional policy responses to social issues and problems have come under increasing scrutiny. Orthodoxies are attacked, conventional wisdoms undermined. In many respects it is those young people in weak bargaining positions who have borne the brunt of these changes. The transition from the family home to independence, from school to work, are periods which have always been fraught with difficulty for many young people - periods of living in low quality accommodation on low incomes or grants in often overcrowded conditions. Typically, however, this was a temporary state of affairs - a short term stepping stone to better quality accommodation as incomes increased and relationships settled. Some fear, however, that those young casualities of the recent period of social and economic change are locked into a set of adverse circumstances which may prove long term rather than temporary. Sharing with parents or roughing it in low quality housing may reflect, increasingly, constraint rather than choice for many young households. There is nothing new in a pattern of housing and employment trajectories among young people which are highly differentiated by gender, class or race. What may be new is the extent to which, at least in some countries, minority experiences appear to be diverging from those of the majority. It is also possible that housing market and labour market adjustments and new policy initiatives will benefit a new group of young people - condemning segments of a previous

FIGURE 1

PROPORTION OF POPULATION AGED 20-24
AND PROPORTION OF UNEMPLOYED 20-24

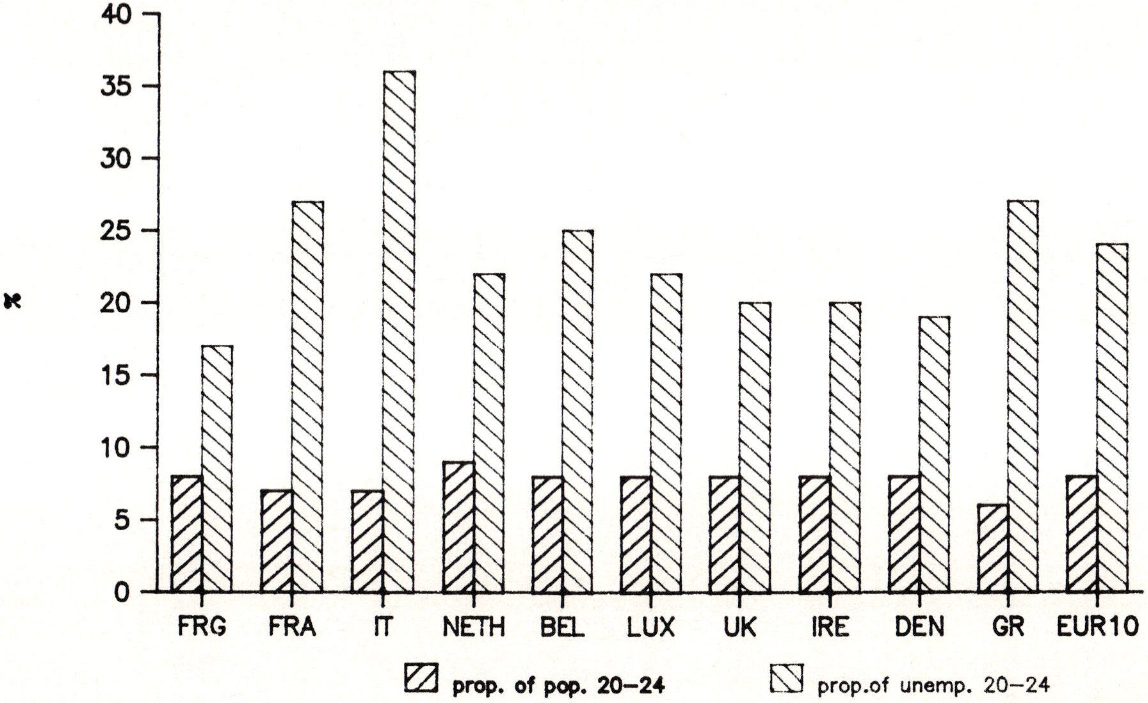

SOURCE:LABOUR FORCE SURVEY (1985)
POPULATION AND SOCIAL CONDITIONS,EUROSTAT

generation to long term unemployment and multi-dimensional marginalisation. Deelstra and Schokkenbroek refer to this 'lost generation' as a group caught in a 'vicious circle':

> The older they become, the more expensive they are for employers. Unemployment also acts as a stigma. An employer will ask himself [sic] why an applicant has not found work sooner. Research reveals that the majority of young people who have not found a job after a year will still not have one three years later. (p 37)

Such a perspective cautions against being mesmerised by a particular stage in the life cycle - it also emphases the <u>importance of those formative stages for young people in the shaping of their lifetime housing and employment histories and their overall life chances.</u>

Population projections also indicate a reduction in the general demographic pressure on labour and housing markets from young age cohorts. As Table II.1 indicates, only Greece shows a marginal increase in the proportion of the population in the 15-24 age group over the next decade. There are, of course, a myriad of problems in interpreting such data. Similar trends do not indicate similar consequences in the different nation states. In the UK, for example, the last decade has seen an unusually large bulge of new entrants to the labour market and the sharp fall is generally regarded positively as relieving pressure on the housing and job markets. In the UK, as in many other European Community countries, policy and political attention is shifting rapidly to the problems of the expanding number of elderly and very elderly people in the population. The Federal Republic of Germany, on the other hand, has experienced a decline in the number of new entrants to the labour market, a trend which looks set to gather momentum in the 1990s. This is one reason why youth unemployment has been less evident there. It has, however, resulted in a shortage of new, young qualified labour market entrants, an increasing imbalance between the economically active and inactive and, for example, personnel deficiencies in the army (Jablonka et al, p 3). Greece, Portugal and Ireland (not shown in Table II) have particularly youthful populations and less buoyant economies. Also, demographic shifts in one age cohort cannot be seen in isolation. Obviously, a declining proportion of younger people could still represent an absolute increase if the population was expanding. More specifically, Jablonka et al point out that in the FRG the shrinking younger cohort may well face increasing competition for housing from the expanding group of 25-30 year olds who tend to be dependent on the same housing market segment (p 3).

There is a further aspect of demographic change in some countries which should also be acknowledged. The age structure of different ethnic groups varies. In the Netherlands, for example, ethnic minorities such as Moluccans, Surinamese and Antilleans have notably younger demographic structures than the majority ethnic group (Deelstra and Schokkenbroek, p 24). In Amsterdam, 25% of young people belong to an ethnic minority. In ten years' time the figure is expected to rise to 35%. In the UK there is a demographic bulge of young people of West Indian origin and, to a lesser extent, of Asian origin. These young black people are more likely to be in semi-skilled and unskilled work and be unemployed or underemployed. A similar trend can be seen in the Federal Republic of Germany where, for example, there is a very high birth rate among Turkish families and a high proportion of young Turks have poor educational and vocational qualifications.

The general point is that shrinking overall numbers of young people in a national population may conceal significant changes in their characteristics - changes which could indicate new housing needs and demands, a varying pattern of new household formation and potentially deeper problems of social, political and economic marginality for some groups.

Leaving the family home

Whilst it is almost universally true that, in Europe at least, young people do leave home, the pattern varies within and between countries. There are stark contrasts between, for example, Greece and the Netherlands. In the former, an exceptionally high number of young people remain in the parental home well into their twenties. Leaving home and getting married are generally synonymous. New household formation among young, single people is of little significance and limited to an affluent minority. For males in the 20-24 age group, only 12.7% are married (1975 figures). Given the low incidence of cohabitation in Greece (de facto, as opposed to de jure marriages) the marriage rate is a reasonable indicator of the significance of the family home for this age cohort. In the Netherlands, by way of contrast, some 75% of young people aged 18-25 live away from their parents and marriage has continued to wane in importance as a means of achieving independence. Such comparisons indicate that if we were concerned solely with the <u>process</u> of new household formation we should focus on different age cohorts in different countries, or at least extend our conception of 'young people'. In this report we have taken a pragmatic view, as did the various consultants, and adopted a flexible view of young people as the situation and discussion demands.

Generally, there are marked gender differences in the age at which young people leave home. Women leave home earlier than men. Various factors account for this. One obvious reason is that women generally marry or cohabit with older men. In the Federal Republic of Germany, however, women also now form the majority of young people living alone (some 53%). One explanation put forward for this is that for young women there is greater need to escape from the parental home in order to gain independence and establish individual adult identity. Thus it is suggested that:

> .... gender specific role expectations of the parents play a role here. Daughters have to reckon with more restrictive attitudes regards personal freedoms, choice of partner and sexuality (see for example Hubner-Funk et al, 1983). Daughters will also be expected, more than sons, to take responsibility for household tasks. (Jablonka et al, p 8)

There are also, however, powerful structural reasons why strong gender differences persist. A feature of social housing, for example, is the priority given within allocation policies to young single parents as opposed to other young single people. Stated simply, pregnancy is often the quickest route to being allocated a dwelling in the social rented sector. Military service in many countries also inhibits and delays the achievement of independence among young men. In Portugal, around 8% of those in the 20-24 age group are in military service. In Greece, some 10-15% of males in the same age group are doing their military service (Kelperis et al, 1985, quoted in Emmanuel, p 10). Bauer and Cuzon also highlight the impact of military service in France as a restraint on the departure of males from the family home. Moreover, males seeking employment at an early age face particular difficulties given the reluctance of employers to take them on before their obligation to undertake military service is fulfilled (p 23).

Unemployment also has a differential impact on males and females. The inability to find work delays the departure from the family home more obviously for males than females. Some caution is required here, however, given the lower propensity of women to register as unemployed, variable participation rates among women in different countries and the general contrasts between the development of capitalist labour markets cross nationally. Nevertheless, some common, if complex, trends are evident. The general rise in youth unemployment has had a disproportionate impact on women. Women are also staying longer in the educational system. Both these factors have tended to contribute to a delayed departure from the family home. Broader social changes have, however, continued to increase general participation rates in the labour market among young women. These factors have contributed to a narrowing of the differences between the sexes, as regards the achievement of residential independence, in the younger age groups (say 18-22). Beyond that, however, the continuing dominance of males in the more highly qualified occupations produces a sharp divergence. In relation to France, Lagree notes that:

> Young women are continuing to strike out independently despite the crisis and the recession in the job market with a steady frequency. Young men, on the other hand, undoubtedly more dependent on having a professional activity, are still more inclined to remain within the family unit. Thus.... the effects of the economic crisis are working in different ways for men and women and the tendencies are even being reversed in relation to the ages of those involved. (Lagree, 1986, quoted in Bauer and Cuzon, p 19)

It should be noted in passing that by northern European standards, labour market participation among young women remains extremely low in Greece and Portugal. In all situations the recession has made women more vulnerable to unemployment and has further inhibited their entry into the labour market. Activity rates for young women aged 20-24 in France at 66% is, however, in sharp contrast to comparable figures for Portugal (21%) and Greece (41%). What is perhaps more surprising is the low activity rates for young males in Greece. Whereas in Portugal dramatic gender differences exist with regard to levels of economic activity - some 80% of males in the 20-24 age group are economically active - in Greece the gender distinction is much less evident. In fact only half of males in the 20-24 age group are labelled officially as economically active. Emmanuel speculates about the reason for this in the following terms:

> It is young men in the 20-24 age group that show, at first glance, a surprisingly limited involvement with the labour market. Does this, in combination with the equally high unemployment rate, indicate restricted opportunities? Nearly 60% of the young men in this group, about 135,000 in 1981, were not seeking employment. A large part of this can be accounted for by other legitimate full-time activities: studying and the army.

But he goes on:

> ....there is some hard evidence that a substantial part of the more young men their twenties - possibly as much as one fifth - remain in some sense 'idle'. (Emmanuel, p 10)

He remains unconvinced, however, of the extent to which low rates of household formation and high levels of 'idleness' can be attributed to lack of employment opportunities "forcing them to fall back on family support". Substantial pressures have however built up since 1981 with rapidly rising levels of youth unemployment due to economic recession and austerity policy measures.

What is evident in all the case studies is the highly differentiated nature of early housing and employment trajectories among young people. Moreover, it is not a simple distinction between the relative ages at which people leave home. Rather it has to be interpreted in terms of <u>choice and constraint</u>. What is consistent is the location of different sub-groups of the young, at different points on the choice/constraint continuum. At one end are typically middle class males in the ethnic majority. Their final departure from the parental home may be delayed by their limited economic resources as they complete their higher education. It is also this group who benefit disproportionately from purpose built student accommodation which in many countries is the only form of housing targeted specifically at young people. In some contexts, in the UK or the FRG for example, it is also this group of well-educated males (and females) for whom the privately rented furnished sector represents a short period of fashionable bohemianism, a temporary stepping stone in low quality accommodation between the parental home and relatively secure and comfortable independence in the housing and labour markets.

At the other extreme are young males and females in the ethnic minorities who may experience longer periods of entrapment in the family home due to dwindling employment opportunities, and more intense discrimination. It is this group who have been most vulnerable to reduced access to social rented housing, cuts in welfare benefits and who have been the greatest casualties of the transformation of employment structures and opportunities. Deelstra and Schokkenbroek refer to:

> A new core .... that remains unaffected legally, financially and in terms of working hours. Around them are forming a number of 'peripheral' positions occupied by the poorly educated, women and ethnic minorities. (p 19)

In countries such as Ireland with relatively small ethnic minorities, social and spatial inequality has unambiguous class dimensions (Ronayne, op cit).

In drawing this section to a close one strong message which comes across from various of the consultants' reports is the centrality of the family as an institution in the current period of social and economic change. Whilst marriage as an institution continues to be of diminishing relevance to many young people, the family remains as a central institution in people's lives. In some countries the extended family continues to provide the social cement of symetrical reciprocity between the generations, notably in Greece, Portugal and Italy. This is a complex area and it is often difficult and probably impossible to disentangle cultural habituation from economic constraint. For example, in Portugal the extended family is a decreasingly important feature of the social structure but there is some indication that more young people are now required to contribute to the overall household income (Mendes, p 7). Di Palma et al also stress the significance of 'component' wages within lower income households. They comment that:

> ....many young people in fact live in families whose economic circumstances are acceptable overall in that they ensure a moderate standard of living for each member of the family but are not sufficient to maintain one or more of their members in living arrangements separate from the original domestic situation, bearing in mind the diseconomies of scale to which this would also lead. (p 34)

Fiscal austerity measures have also tended to transfer a greater share of the burden of supporting young people from the state to the family. Conservative ideologies stress the importnce of the role of the family in caring for both the dependent young and old. Bauer and Cuzon refer to the essential role of the family in providing "the long-term young unemployed with the means of survival". They go on, however, to suggest that the young unemployed who "are no longer constrained by the demands of regular employment .... threaten the already fragile balance of their families, which are the most vulnerable ones" (pp 68, 69).

This view of the 'stressed' family is also taken up by Di Palma et al in the Italian context. They describe a situation in which traditional bonds of reciprocity within the enlarged family unit are being eroded at the same time as the family has had to reassert its role in providing support and assistance for family members:

> The subsequent crisis in the welfare state arising from the need to contain public spending, has deprived the family of many of the types of support and assistance which the reforms instituted, leaving it in essence to make its own way in a society in which services are often available, but nobody knows where or under what conditions, or in which there is little confidence in the quality of the services provided. (p 29)

It would seem that the post war growth of welfare institutions diminished the relationships of dependency between the older and younger generations. This was clearly more evident in some countries than in others and strong contrasts exist between northern and southern Europe in this respect. Whereas the vast majority of young people in the UK, the Netherlands and the Federal Republic of Germany live independently of their parents by the age of 24, the family home remains the dominant form of accommodation for young people in Italy, Portugal and Greece. Indeed, the majority of young people in the 20-24 age group in France still live with their parents. Taking a broader view, however, it is apparent that a greater dependence among young people on family support in all its forms accentuates the unequal resources available to families within different social groups. <u>When the attainment of independence is increasingly reliant on family support this will favour inevitably those young people in families in the strongest social and economic situations.</u>

Young people in the labour market

Entering the labour market is always a difficult stage in any individual's life. It usually involves a swift and marked contrast with school or university life. It may involve a fall in housing and living standards, departure from the family home and a move away from the familiar surroundings of childhood. From what has been said in previous sections it is evident that for the majority of young people these changes are unlikely to occur simultaneously. The extent to which the various 'transitional' changes do coincide varies among countries and among different groups of young people within countries. Race, class and gender divisions are associated with distinctive early lifetime trajectories into the housing and labour markets. And in some countries the break between education and work is far more clear cut than in others. Whereas in northern Europe the majority of young people expect and do attain residential independence at an early age, it is more common in countries such as Italy, Greece and France to remain in the family home well beyond the teenage years.

Patterns of social inequality, housing market processes, cultural norms, educational systems and broader contrasts in the material conditions of different societies combine in complex ways to produce different transitional processes for young people and different outcomes. As in all comparative studies it is important to acknowledge that apparently similar outcomes may be the consequence of different processes. Equally, similar processes may produce different outcomes. For example the common observation that young people are apparently staying longer in the family home is clearly subject to quite different interpretation depending upon class and gender and the national context in which that observation is being made. Nevertheless, we can draw out a number of underlying processes which have affected employment opportunities in recent years and the ways they have impacted particularly on young people. Many of these changes have already been commented upon in earlier discussion. This section seeks merely to elaborate upon the principal issues involved.

Young people are staying in the educational system longer. Higher skill levels, higher qualifications are required in order to compete effectively in the labour market. There is also a strong element of what has been referred to as 'qualification explosion' whereby, for example, jobs which previously required school leaving certificates now require university degrees or diplomas. In other words, the ante is always being raised and qualifications are being progressively devalued. Longer educational participation among young people is also associated with economic development. Conversely, perhaps, it is also associated with a lack of employment opportunities. Deelstra and Schokkenbroek, for example, refer to school as a 'parking place'. "Pupils stay at school longer because they have no prospect of finding a job" (p 10).

The general impression is that the temporal connections between the completion of education, marriage/cohabitation, leaving home and entering the labour market have become more diverse and for some young people, more problematic. As Jablonka et al observe:

> Different social groups .... finish their education at very different ages; whereas half of all students are older than 25, young people generally finish their vocational training by the age of 20. Nor is there a close connection between completing education and beginning work; between leaving the parental home and marriage or between marriage and having children. (p 4)

Similarly, Di Palma et al comment that in Italy:

> There are many young people who start working while continuing to study, and many who, although they have already started working, continue with their education, albeit with delays. (p 4)

It is also the case, however, that many young people in Italy enter the labour market between the ages of 14 and 19 - some at a very early age. Obviously the age of entry is influenced by statutory regulations regarding minimum school leaving age - and this varies between countries. A more fundamental and more general issue which is raised at least implicity in a number of the consultants' reports relates to a growing polarisation between the mass of young people who are staying longer in the educational system and significant minorities who drop out of the system at an early age. The likelihood of finding employment and the nature of that employment is linked unambiguously and unsurprisingly to levels of educational achievement. And levels of educational achievement continue to have strong class, gender and race dimensions (see, for example, Ronayne pp 27, 28). In the context of the Netherlands, Deelstra and Schokkenbroek refer to the "not inconsiderable proportion of young people who leave school poorly educated and without any kind of certificate" (p 7). Later they refer to a 'fringe group' of young drop outs who are in danger of becoming socially and culturally isolated (p 30).

This pervasive view of polarisation among young people on a number of dimensions can be linked to the profound changes which have occurred in the overall structure of employment. In some cases this relates to the shift from manufacturing to service sector employment and the consequences of that development for new skill requirements, the gender composition of the workforce, shifting patterns of labour force entry and the general impact on youth unemployment. In other cases, such as in Portugal, Greece and Ireland, where the historical patterns of industrialisation and proletarianisation have been rather different, the issues revolve more directly around rampant urbanisation, the growing salience of waged labour and the ruptures which have occurred in traditional patterns of family life and informal support systems. In a rather more sophisticated and structurally bedded version of the cycle of the deprivation thesis, Rothman and O'Connell have referred to the transformation of the class structure of Ireland in the following terms:

> By 1971 the new hierarchy of class positions was apparent. The value of various forms of economic resources had shifted, changing the balance of advantage and disadvantage associated with particular skills, qualifications and businesses.... Even in 1979, a substantial share of the workforce was in residual classes stranded in the course of industrial development, especially farmers on marginal holdings and labourers without skills. People in these marginal categories have little opportunity to transfer to the more favourably placed categories; their children's chances are little better, perpetuating marginality within families. (Rothman and O'Connell, p 72, quoted in Ronayne, p 15)

Sectoral changes in the structure of employment have had particular effects on the age at which young people enter the labour force, the skills and length of training they require and the gender composition of the workforce. The shift in overall employment from manufacturing to service sectors (and from agricultural to manufacturing/service sector employment) has tended to raise the average age at which young people start work (Di Palma et al, p 4). And whereas women are virtually absent from agriculture, those in waged labour are heavily concentrated in the service sector (Ronayne, p 28; Emmanuel, p 12). Typically, it is industry and construction which have been most severely affected by recession and economic restructuring. And it is these sectors which historically have been the key employment sectors for male, blue-collar work. Young working class males therefore have been particular casualties of recent economic changes. On the other hand, women have been participating at ever higher rates in the growing service sector (albeit often in insecure, part-time work) but have been subject to increased gender discrimination in the labour market and growing social pressure to remain 'in the home' as labour market conditions have grown more adverse. Whilst there has been a marked and general 'feminisation' of work, there has also been increased gender competition for scarce employment.

Flexibility has become a key word in descriptions and analyses of changes in the nature of employment conditions, recruitment strategies and the broader reshaping of the sphere of work. Translated into everyday experience this has meant the growth of more casual and insecure forms of employment with part-time and fixed-term contracts replacing long-term, permanent jobs. In the academic literature this is often conceptualised in terms of a core-periphery model of labour market segmentation with an increased polarisation between those in secure, well-paid, high status employment and those on the casualised fringes. Whilst such a description captures usefully one dimension of growing social division it is generally acknowledged that the pattern is in fact rather more complex and varies between sectors and between countries.

Nevertheless, it is evident that many young people have not only had to contend with rising unemployment but also a deterioration in the terms and conditions of work which is on offer. For those who do not experience unemployment on leaving school or college the alternative may be a succession of casual jobs, on short term contracts or on state training schemes. Bauer and Cuzon, for example, note an expanding category within the French working population who alternate between temporary work and unemployment, with young people being particularly prominent (p 12). Uncertainty and insecurity have become more commonplace in the early work experiences of those young people who are in weaker bargaining positions in the labour market. The fear is that for some this may represent more than a transitional stage. In societies where access to housing and other resources is increasingly dependent on credit rating, terms of employment are of some importance. Moreover, Ronayne notes that:

> ....in contrast to young people from middle class backgrounds, many young people from working class backgrounds who do manage to obtain employment will by virtue of a combination of their lower levels of educational achievement and lack of family contacts with employment opportunities in the primary sector of the labour market typically find themselves in jobs that are insecure, low paid, offer little or no promotion opportunities and with poor working conditions in general. (p 24)

We have already stressed on a number of occasions in the report that rising unemployment had a disproportionate impact on young people. This is uncontroversial and unambiguous and need only be reiterated briefly at this point in order to draw out the principal dimensions and variations involved. Figure II.2 compares the proportion of populations in the 20-24 age category with the proportions out of work in that group. Unemployment figures are notoriously difficult to compare cross nationally because of differences in definition and recording practices. Nevertheless, the general pattern is clear and consistent. Young people are particularly vulnerable to unemployment. It has, however, already been stressed that the experience and incidence of unemployment and underemployment is highly varied spatially and socially. Some examples serve to illustrate this general observation. Jablonka et al comment that youth unemployment in the FRG was generally most acute in the 1970s. Since then it has become more noticeably concentrated among "women, foreigners and older workers". In December 1986 the general rate of unemployment was 8.9%. For women it was 10.3% and for non-nationals 14.1%. They also note that the general rate of unemployment is "around twice as high in the structurally weak regions of North Germany than it is in South Germany" (p 15). Similarly strong spatial variations can be found in other countries. In France, the unemployment rate among job-seekers aged under 25 varied from 38% in the depressed regions of Nord-Pas-de-Calais and Haute-Normandie to 25% in the more prosperous Paris region (it should be noted in passing that there is not a consistent relationship between the youth rate and the general rate of unemployment in the various regions, Bauer and Cuzon, p 32). There is also a strong north-south dimension to youth unemployment in the UK with a marked dislocation between employment opportunities and access to housing (Burton, Forrest and Stewart, 1987).

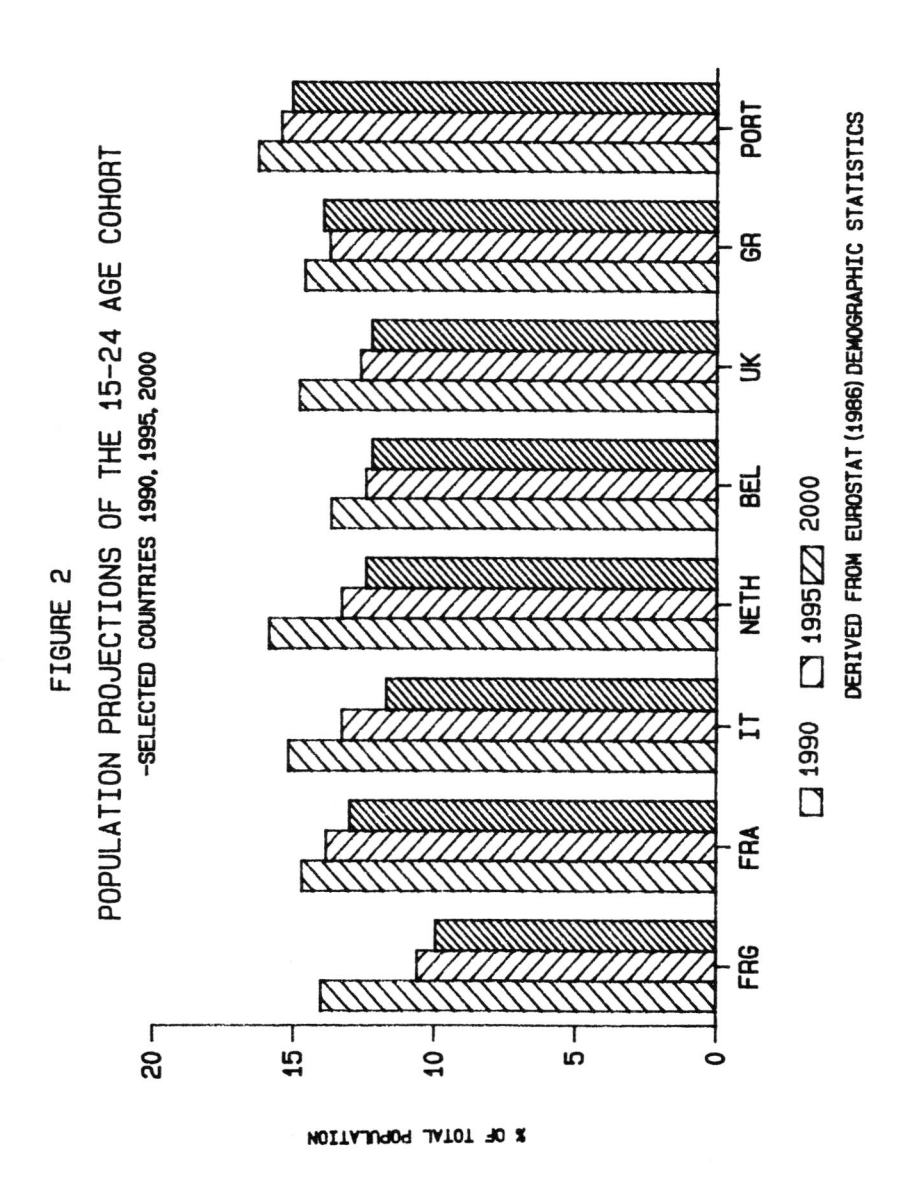

FIGURE 2
POPULATION PROJECTIONS OF THE 15-24 AGE COHORT
-SELECTED COUNTRIES 1990, 1995, 2000

□ 1990 □ 1995 ▨ 2000

DERIVED FROM EUROSTAT (1986) DEMOGRAPHIC STATISTICS

As regards gender differences Deelstra and Schokkenbroek show that girls are more often unemployed for a long period than boys (p 22). More generally they indicate that young women are "less geared to the labour market in their choice of post-compulsory education", that for women, more so than for men, "the family is a valid alternative to unemployment" and that typically women make work outside the home "dependent on the time needed for the family" (op cit, p 23). They also note that "in the construction of housing no account is taken of the possibility of combining home and work" (p 23).

Whilst the level and duration of unemployment has strong class dimension in Ireland, there are also marked ethnic differences in countries such as the UK, the FRG, the Netherlands and France. In the UK the level of unemployment is most acute within the black population (Burton, Forrest and Stewart, 1987). In the Netherlands the general rate of unemployment for those in the 15-24 age group is 26% (1986 figures). Among the same age group in the Turkish and Moroccan community the rates are 45% and 47% respectively (Deelstra and Schokkenbroek, p 26).

All these developments in the labour market combine to produce a general deterioration in the economic position of young people. More young people are unemployed. More are unemployed for longer. There is greater instability, uncertainty and insecurity. The impact of recession and economic change has been felt generally and disproportionately by young people but it has been highly uneven in its effect. In many countries the general and youth unemployment rates have begun to fall. Again this may be highly uneven in its social and spatial impact, may reflect (to some extent at least) 'administrative' changes in the recording procedures and may camouflage a continuing deterioration in the financial position of those sub-groups on training schemes and in insecure and low paid employment. Young people's incomes have been falling in comparison with older workers over the last few years. This has been mainly a consequence of the impact of unemployment and the general renegotiation of labour relations. To some extent, however, it has been the direct result of government policies - as in the UK, France, the Netherlands, Italy and the FRG. Unemployment benefits have been squeezed and stricter eligibility rules applied. Rights to unemployment benefit are typically dependent on having been employed. Jablonka et al show that just over half of those unemployed below the age of 20 are <u>eligible</u>

for unemployment assistance or benefit. For 'foreigners' under 20 the figure drops to 22% (pp 16, 17). Although there is a statutory minimum wage in the Netherlands this has been reduced significantly over the last five years - as have all income support measures for young people (Deelstra and Schokkenbroek, pp 37-38). As governments seek to squeeze expenditure on benefits for low priority groups it is young single people who tend to suffer most - and their parents, if they have any, who have to provide alternative financial support. A recent survey in France, for example, indicated that a fifth of young people (16-24) were receiving financial assistance from parents (Bauer and Cuzon, p 56). Young people are it seems having to fall back increasingly on the family as a support system in the absence of employment and housing opportunities. Also, as has already been mentioned, the wage of the adult child(ren) is often a vital component in the household income of families in marginal economic circumstances.

Some commentators have suggested that wider forms of informal support are developing as survival mechanisms for the young. By definition, of course, the 'hidden' or 'informal' economy is a difficult area to explore. General research on this area has tended to suggest that the formal and informal sectors are rather closely connected and that its role as a support system for the unemployed may have been greatly exaggerated. Nevertheless, common sense and common observation suggests that it is a source of income for some young people. It also links to work on crime and deviancy among the young. Ronayne (1987), for example, refers to research on this area which "clearly documents the role of social deprivation in the lives of young people for whom crime has become not only a source of income but also, in the absence of other opportunities, a 'lifestyle'" (p 31). It is in this context where concerns about employment and housing difficulties for groups within the young population link to broader policy and political debates regarding social deviancy, social exclusion and social cohesion. When the system seems unable to deliver, when the transition from adolescence to adult status seems littered with insurmountable obstacles, when the problems seem long rather than short term, the understandable disillusionment can lead to an abandonment of the normal and socially acceptable forms of coping and surviving. Whilst it would be wrong to overemphasise this development there does appear to be a sizeable minority among the young who have 'given up' on, or been denied, the traditional routes of transition.

Housing opportunities for young people

We have already mapped out the broad issues of relevance to a consideration of the housing opportunities of young people in urban Europe. The preceding discussion emphasised <u>the need to look well beyond the specifics of housing policies and housing markets to understand the housing situation of young people</u>. Moreover, whilst a number of common processes have been identified, and indeed some general trends, there are enormous social, spatial and cultural variations which cautions against oversimplification and overgeneralisation.

Given the particular focus of this study and the space constraints, it would be inappropriate to enter into an elaborate discussion of the different structures of housing provision which exist in different countries. General accounts of this kind, both theoretical and descriptive, are available elsewhere (see, for example, Ball et al, 1988; Burton et al, 1986; Kroes et al, 1988). It is appropriate, however, to examine, albeit briefly, some of the principal developments in housing provision which are affecting the early stages of young people's housing histories.

In previous sections we have discussed broad demographic trends, particularly in relation to pattern of household formation, marriage and cohabitation rates, the general though uneven trend towards smaller households and the broader shift towards more elderly populations. It has been stressed that particular demographic patterns do not have inevitable or necessary effects as regards changing housing demands. The implications which flow from, say, a projected decline of the 15-24 age cohort will vary according to a range of factors. These include the overall pattern of wealth and income distribution, the pattern and level of unemployment, the demographic changes occurring in relation to other age cohorts and the existing pattern of housing opportunities. Aspects of employment and income are, of course, central to understanding housing problems and opportunities in general. Indeed, many commentators would argue that we need look no further in order to understand the nature of housing disadvantage among certain groups of young people. Bauer and Cuzon stress that problems do not derive from an overall housing shortage. "The essential factor is a shortage of money, mostly due to unemployment" (p 2).

It is undoubtedly the case that regardless of context, the relatively affluent young have few housing problems. It is equally true that those in the weakest bargaining positions face a range of housing constraints whether we are discussing the UK, Portugal or the Netherlands. The structure of housing markets do not however simply reflect patterns of disadvantage which may be rooted elsewhere. They act in many ways to ameliorate or exacerbate inequalities. Living on a particular estate or in a particular kind of housing may label young people in negative ways. Being a home owner may be an essential component of credit worthiness and a route to money gains in the housing market. Conversely, those excluded from particular tenures may also be excluded from the mainstream of social consumption. In the strict sense, these kinds of issues may be regarded as epiphenomenal but there is no doubt that patterns of housing advantage and disadvantage take on distinctive forms according to the different structures of provision which exist in different countries.

Ignoring the finer detail for a moment and indeed some of the major social, economic, political and cultural differences it may be useful at this stage, to draw out the principal issues in housing with regard to younger households. The list below highlights the points made in a number of the consultants' reports as well as reiterating in summary form some of the issues and processes referred to earlier.

(a) There is a marked restructuring of the urban environment with the traditional users of lower quality, lower cost inner city areas facing greater dangers of <u>displacement</u>. Younger people and particularly younger, single people are strongly represented in this group. As inner areas are gentrified and become increasingly the domain of the more affluent, young people may be pushed outwards into environments which are less well suited to their needs.

(b) Current processes of urban renewal are accelerating the decline of privately rented housing. This contraction of the private rental market has a long and complicated history in a number of countries. Much of it is attributable to the rates of return available on investment elsewhere and on the structures of housing subsidies which have tended to favour other forms of tenure, most notably owner occupation. As the privately rented sector has become increasingly associated with lower income groups such as elderly people, students and other young single people the central dilemma of rent control has become more acute. Those groups who most need the flexibility and easy access of private renting can least afford to pay a market rent. Decontrol prices certain groups out of the market or alternatively puts pressure on state income support subsidies. The imposition or reimposition of controls leads to further shortage and disinvestment.

(c) One symptom of retrenchment and recession has been a fiscal squeeze which has affected disproportionately those groups in low priority categories such as young, single people. In some cases income levels of young people in general have declined in real terms. More consistently, young people have continued to be excluded from targeted housing and other income support subsidies, have become increasingly ineligible through rule changes or changed circumstances (eg more young people living at home for longer periods) or have experienced reductions in the value of the benefits for which they do qualify.

(d) The reduced effective demand among many younger groups has been made more acute by a reorientation towards market solutions in the housing sphere in general and, in particular, the promotion of home ownership by governments. This reorientation towards market processes and away from direct forms of state provision is symptomatic of the squeeze on public expenditure but also reflects a widespread disillusionment with past forms of state intervention in the housing market. There is a marked political and ideological retreat from the direct provision of social housing and forms of housing support for lower income households which are not compatible with private sector imperatives. Whilst in some countries fiscal pressures have eased there is little indication of a change of policy direction.

(e) The increased emphasis on promoting individual home ownership in national housing policies favours inevitably the older, more established households. To varying degrees home ownership is beyond the financial means of the average young person. Whilst housing finance institutions in some countries have adjusted policies to enable the sharing among young single people of mortgage responsibilities there are other issues of mobility and access which tend to make home ownership <u>socially</u> inappropriate for younger, transient groups in the population.

(f) Whilst the 'decomposition' of the extended family is less marked in Southern Mediterranean countries with a strong Catholic tradition, the general trend is towards smaller households, more single person households and earlier household formation. There is a consistent view of a mismatch between the <u>physical</u> structure of dwelling stocks and contemporary housing needs. There is a shortage of small dwelling units. How far relative and absolute dwelling shortages contribute to delayed household formation and longer periods living with parents is extremely difficult to measure and varies according to cultural and economic context. For the majority of younger, single people in the countries included in this study the parental home remains the predominant form of residence. For some this reflects constraint rather than choice, and is subject to different interpretations in different cultures. Nevertheless, there is a clear if uneven association between the level of economic development and the average age at which young people leave the parental home. And there are <u>clear indications that income, employment and housing factors have combined to make that transitional stage more difficult at the present time.</u>

(g) In countries with relatively large public housing sectors (eg UK, Ireland, France and Germany) privatisation measures have (or will) either transferred sections of the public housing stock to the owner occupied sector or have removed dwellings from subsidy arrangements. This erosion of the public housing sector has a number of consequences for young people. In high demand housing markets it tends to increase competition for rented housing among lower income groups in general and reduces flexibility in allocation policies. Whilst young couples, families and single parents have been catered for by public housing, young single people have generally been excluded or afforded low priority. In some situations falling demand for public housing from families and more mature households has opened up the possibility of more allocations to younger people. Privatisation, however, reduces the scope for more flexible allocation criteria. Conversely, high vacancy rates and potential public housing surpluses in lower demand areas has opened up public housing to young people. Social room letting has been introduced in the Netherlands. Some local authorities in the UK allocate dwellings to unrelated, young sharers. Often, however, there are problems of dwelling type and location. Large dwellings or dwellings on peripheral estates are often unsuitable for young people.

(h) There has been a noted increase in young homelessness although homelessness definitionally and conceptually does not 'travel' well. Homelessness can take many forms according to age and gender and there are a variety of routes and responses. And it may cross national boundaries as in the case of young, migrant workers. Moreover, a number of the reports have stressed the need to regard 'homelessness' as much more than simply a lack of shelter but more broadly in terms of having a secure place in society, being within the mainstream rather than on the margins. What is evident is that there has been an increase in the number of young people living on the margins and in housing terms this marginality takes a number of forms. It may refer to female single parents on isolated peripheral estates, young people living in hostels as well as those sleeping rough on the streets. Living on the streets is only one of a myriad of forms of young homelessness. Much of it remains concealed. Whilst in northern Europe there has been an increase in <u>overt</u> homelessness among young people in urban areas, in other countries, where the family remains the dominant provider of accommodation, homelessness of this form is much less common and is more likely to be seen in pathological (ie deviancy, drugs) rather than structural terms (ie lack of jobs, cheap housing). Squatting similarly takes on quite different connotations in say the Netherlands where it is semi-institutionalised and associated with alternative lifestyles than in Portugal or Greece where 'squatting' refers to peripheral shanty type settlements and illegal developments. Where there are ample supplies of cheap, bad housing, homelessness, in the strictest interpretation of the term (eg rooflessness), is unlikely to be a major problem.

In this section we have drawn out some of the principal housing issues in relation to young people which appear to have some general currency at a European level. There has been no attempt to deal with the finer details of policy, the major differences among national housing systems or with specific housing initiatives for young people. These are dealt with later in the report. It is perhaps unnecessary to re-emphasise that common themes and issues do not necessarily have common causes or consequences or that the housing histories of young people are highly differentiated. Moreover, whilst a study of this kind highlights the problems faced by particular groups in the housing and labour markets, it is important to stress that the majority of young people negotiate the transition from dependence to independence relatively unproblematically. Their housing opportunities have generally expanded over the last decade or so and their housing conditions have improved.

Nevertheless, there would seem to be a <u>growing dislocation between housing and labour market process which is having a particular impact on young people</u>. Whilst <u>flexibility</u> in the labour market and the general impact of profound economic restructuring is tending to polarise employment conditions and opportunities and creating greater insecurity and uncertainty in the job market, structures of housing provision have become increasingly <u>inflexible</u>. Generally, young people are more mobile and have more limited resources than the population as a whole. In recent years those young people in the weakest bargaining positions have experienced less job security, rising unemployment and underemployment and reduced effective demand. They confront, however, a housing market where access to credit, credit worthiness and job security are if anything more important than ever. Young people require forms of housing provision which offer relatively easy access, mobility and low entry costs. Home ownership is not the ideal tenure in those respects. And the contraction of alternative routes to residential independence for young people is particularly serious in situations where the system of housing finance makes early access to home ownership extremely difficult. In the Federal Republic of Germany, for example, house price to income ratios are very high and "house purchase occurs at a time when for the children the process of gaining independence from the parental home is already beginning" (Jablonka et al, p 29). Similarly, in Greece, with a high overall level of home ownership access to that tenure comes relatively late in life and is the culmination of a protracted effort to accumulate savings and is heavily dependent on intergenerational transfers of wealth:

> For the average young household, the achievement of owner occupation by its own means <u>even</u> in the case where it succeeds in receiving a mortgage loan, is clearly beyond realistic consideration. (Emmanuel, p 24)

In contrast, the UK has a highly developed owner occupied market and widespread access to mortgage finance. Leaving aside the differential pattern of house price inflation with rapidly escalating house prices in southern England, young people can and do enter the owner occupied market at an early age. Some 38% of heads of household in the 20-24 age group are in the owner occupied sector. A rather different profile, however, is evident for the young unemployed who remain heavily dependent on the parental home and a shrinking public housing sector.

Looking towards the future, and particularly 1992, it is likely that greater harmonisation of financial systems and an opening up of financial markets in Europe will create greater uniformity in the structure and pattern of housing finance. This may well move countries generally nearer the system which prevails in Britain with relatively easy access to high percentage-of-value loans. Indeed this would seem meritable if home ownership continues to be promoted as the preferred housing policy option and if it is to be extended to lower income groups and younger people. Whether or not this is a desirable development and compatible with the needs and aspirations of young people is a matter for debate.

In concluding this chapter it is appropriate to make brief reference to the way in which the housing problems of young people are constructed and interpreted. It is for example evident that the view that this particular group have specific problems and require specific policy measures is somewhat unfamiliar in some national contexts. This is particularly true where general housing problems remain serious and widespread. In Lisbon and Oporto it is estimated that 170,000 families are living in unsatisfactory and overcrowded conditions (Mendes, 1987). And southern European countries generally have lower housing standards, more pervasive housing problems and more limited resources. Whilst there is widespread recognition (and some specific policies) of the needs of young <u>couples</u> a preoccupation with the particular needs of young single people could be regarded as something of a distraction from the more major tasks at hand.

This relates to a further issue, namely the role of the family and the parental home. Housing aspirations and expectations of young people differ markedly among the countries under consideration in this study. The differences relate to the material conditions and cultural norms of different societies. At the heart of this study is a concern with social cohesion, social integration and the problems arising in the transition from youth to adult status. It is evident however that a lack of opportunities for younger people to achieve early independence cannot be interpreted as a 'problem' in a straightforward and universal way. Emmanuel, for example, makes the point that in Greece:

> living with the family and, more generally, being dependent on family support is part of the whole network of family relationships and the mutual obligations involved. It has obvious benefits as well as costs for the young .... There are a lot of people that would react violently to any idea of replacing the main functions of this sytem with social welfare apparatus or, for the more well-off, a friendly bank manager. (p 32)

Considerations of this nature take us into complex and dangerous territory and certainly in the context of the UK would be linked to political ideologies which promote 'family values' and reduced welfare support. It does, however, serve as a reminder that the 'problem' and its 'solution' does not simply revolve around the ability or otherwise of young people to leave home at an early age. Rather it is about constraint and marginality and the extent to which specific sub-groups of the young face a future which is likely to be increasingly divergent from the cultural norms and material circumstances of the majority.

CHAPTER 4: RESPONSES TO THE HOUSING PROBLEMS FACED BY YOUNG PEOPLE

This chapter looks at the range of responses to the housing problems faced by young people in the nine countries studied. We had hoped, originally, to be able to make a highly systematic comparison of the different levels of response in each country, in other words to look at national level state policy responses, the response of national non-government agencies, sub-national government agencies and local level initiatives. However, a number of factors have made this impossible to achieve in practice. First, not all the national case studies covered the same range of responses. In France, Italy, the Netherlands and the Federal Republic of Germany both national and local level responses were studied. In England this was also the case although the local case studies were conducted in less detail. In Greece, Portugal and Ireland the analysis was restricted to the national level while for Spain it focused primarily on Barcelona.

Second, because national perceptions of the nature and scale of the problems facing young people vary, so too do the types of responses. This is compounded by national variations in the organisation of government, nationally and sub-nationally, and other delivery systems associated with the churches or voluntary sector groups. Finally, although all the research teams worked to a common brief and theoretical framework, a significant degree of discretion was encouraged to enable each team to pursue those aspects which appeared to them to be of most relevance and interest.

Notwithstanding these comments the rest of this chapter describes, on a country by country basis, the local case study areas and something of the range of responses to the housing problems faced by young people. In each case national level responses will be presented before those developed at the local level.

Italy

At the national level policy responses directed at young people are framed by four general aims. First, to increase job opportunities for young people in concert with EEC and OECD initiated local job creation schemes. Second, to promote vocational training for young people and thereby to increase their cultural horizons and their knowledge of foreign languages. Third, to establish local centres and units which deal with the problems faced by disabled young people and finally to establish reception communities to treat young people with drug addiction problems.

As Di Palma et al point out:

> At present Italy has no policies with the direct intention of solving the accommodation problem for young people. (p 44)

However, some set aside provision is now made from public housing built entirely or partly with public funds. Along with elderly people, young couples benefit from this set aside but it is tied more to their status as a 'couple' than to their age as:

> .... the family unit made up of only one member (whether young or old) is ignored by Italian housing policy. (p 44)

Young people receive attention from 'indirect' housing policies only if they belong to the 'protected categories' under the headings of the right to study (students) or social welfare (former members of therapeutic communities, former drug addicts, tramps, orphans etc). Outside these categories the problem of homelessness among young people is not felt collectively at the national level and remains a submerged problem.

Also at the national level, but outside the state sector, the voluntary sector is tending to take responsibility in a variety of ways for increasingly large areas of welfare, including aid for marginalised young people.

Religious organisations continue to play an important role in providing young people with support and, in some cases, accommodation. Most large cities with universities have some form of reception centre or hostel run by religious organisations. In Rome for example there are 102 hostels offering accommodation to students and other groups of young people. Of these 88 are for women only and 14 for men. 70 of these are exclusively for use by students. Di Palma et al suggest that a substantial number of women students solve their accommodation problems by working as au pairs with families.

In recent years the voluntary sector in Italy, associated primarily with religious groups, has launched a vast range of measures for young people defined as 'marginal'. This group includes drug addicts, children who have run away from home, foreign immigrants, homeless people, young unmarried mothers and disabled people who are not catered for by traditional institutions. The measures include information centres in the larger urban areas, employment initiatives especially manufacturing co-operatives and residential premises. The latter are geared primarily to providing accommodation but also aim to provide an environment in which young people can regain their motivation and begin to play a more active role in society. A recent survey by Caffarelli (quoted in Di Palma et al, op cit) identified some 386 such residential communities throughout Italy but with a marked bias towards the northern regions. The relationship between these communities and the local authorities varies considerably. In some cases the relationship is very close and young people are referred by the district or area social service office. In other areas there is no contact whatsoever between the communities and the local authorities.

The local case studies were selected on the basis of a north-south distinction, where the south is an area of relative poverty and the north one of relative prosperity. Bologna in the north was chosen because of its affluence and its tradition of well developed and effective social policies, as Di Palma et al note:

> .... thanks to particularly able and enlightened authorities, the city has set up a major network of collective structures, both at the city and the district level, which have made it possible for the population as a whole to live in satisfactory conditions. (p 56)

In the south Naples was chosen as an area faced with major problems of social degradation, unemployment and disorganised local government. In terms of various indicators of economic performance, health and social/cultural conditions, Naples consistently occupies a place near the bottom of a rank order of Italian provinces.

These areas were not chosen to reflect the two extremes of the Italian situation with the assumption that the national average lies equidistant from both. Nor do they illustrate the diversity present in Italian cities. Rather Bologna and Naples were chosen to show how different socio-economic contexts and different forms of municipal intervention effect the opportunities available to young people. On this basis Di Palma et al argue that in Bologna, in contrast to Naples, the greater tradition of administrative efficiency and social solidarity has led to more effective solutions being developed in response to young people's housing problems.

This is not to suggest that young people in the north have virtually no problems or that the problems they do face are receiving an adequate response. Rather it is that in the south the problems are greater, more complex and hence more difficult to solve. It is possible, indeed likely, that this will lead to greater migration by young people who no longer expect to stay in the area in which their original family lived. While the conditions and opportunities in the less prosperous areas may not be very good the case study of Bologna demonstrated the inadequacy of many policies developed under more favourable conditions. This does not bode well for young people who move to more prosperous areas in an attempt to improve, inter alia, their housing prospects.

At the commune level in Naples and Bologna the following types of 'Youth Project' have been initiated: Information centres; Press centres; Training and work schemes (not in Naples!); Social and cultural projects and schemes for the rehabilitation of deviant youths. In all categories there are more projects in Bologna than in Naples, and more have actually been launched than are in the process of being prepared. As there is no national legal framework for social welfare provision, regional laws regulate the measures devised by communes and other forms of local authority in respect of particular age groups.

Bologna has some 437,000 residents of whom approximately 86,000 are aged between 15 and 29. It is estimated that by 1996 the age structure will have changed dramatically as the number of elderly people rises and the number of children and young people falls - up 12,000 and down 61,000 respectively.

The region of Emilia Romagna is responsible for planning the provision of social welfare facilities throughout the area, whilst at the commune level - the city of Bologna for example - there is less scope for action. Nevertheless, Bologna once heralded as the capital of the Italian welfare state has been playing an increasing role in relation to young people. The Youth Projects described above have played an important part but have not become heavily involved in supporting accommodation schemes. The city currently funds a number of halfway houses which help young people who want to leave home but do not have the means to do so. The Youth Project has not yet supported this initiative which is in fact the only public initiative in Bologna which helps young people to achieve independent living. Other measures which seek to improve living conditions are directed at specific groups of people such as students, the disabled, drug addicts and so on. The fact that the users are young is not as important as the fact that they are students, disabled and drug addicts.

Young people as such do not appear near the top of any priority lists operated by the commune in respect of housing allocations. Elderly people, those with handicaps and those on low incomes are ranked highly and as one commune official said: "Young people find it difficult to accumulate all these misfortunes" (quoted in Di Palma et al). It is also suggested that families display a greater willingness to take back young people who may have left home than they show to elderly members of the family who run into housing difficulties. This is then used to explain the fact that elderly people are more likely to be the beneficiaries of commune housing policy measures.

Students constitute a significant proportion of the youthful population of Italian cities. The University of Bologna had almost 60,000 students in the 1985/86 academic year of whom almost 16,000 were resident within the city itself. An agency supported by the commune, the Azienda, provides 1,594 places for students at present and also makes a small number of grants available as well.

Other policy measures are directed at 'marginalised' young people by the Commune Office for Social Policy, local health units (USLs), district commissions and by authorised private organisations. They include 14 communities for minors without parents, half of which are managed privately and an additional eight run by religious organisations.

One initiative of note is an experimental group flat for minors set up jointly by the Ministry of Justice, the Commune and one of the USLs. This has 10 beds and seeks to provide an alternative to prison for young offenders. Similarly an Emergency Group is operating in the same area and providing accommodation in a small flat for the 48-hour detention period in cases where young people are picked up by the police and have no credentials.

Of the other groups described as marginalised the following provision exists: a group of nuns provides accommodation for young unmarried mothers in the city centre; a hostel is run by three workers funded by the Commune on behalf of young people who are poor; ex convicts may be offered temporary accommodation by staff at a reception centre run by a social worker and educational specialist.

Not only have the traditionally high levels of unemployment in Naples had a disproportionate effect on young people but the earthquake of November 1980 destroyed 40,000 dwellings and added to the local housing crisis. The inner city area has been losing population and there is now a significant level of vacancy. At the same time pressure is growing on the housing stock of surrounding areas as people move out:

> Young people in Naples have problems of marginalisation, deviant behaviour and integration which are more critical than in other areas of the country. (Di Palma et al, p 67)

These problems of scarcity, decay and natural disaster have been compounded by chronic deficiencies in local administrative and managerial capacities. A series of reforms have been initiated to regenerate these capacities - as well as the city itself! Nevertheless, our colleagues found no policy measures directed at the accommodation problems faced by young people, except where the young people are also at risk or considered to be deviant in some way.

It was noted, however, that in Naples there is a serious problem relating to delinquent minors. According to a recent survey there are almost 5,000 minors in Naples working for the Camorra as heroin dealers (CENSIS 1986 quoted in Di Palma et al).

Among the more interesting responses to these problems are two initiatives of the regional level of government. The first is a multi-functional youth centre supported by the Regional Board for Social Welfare and Vocational Training. In co-operation with other local government bodies and USLs this centre provides a range of support services to young people including accommodation. The second initiative is still at the planning stage but aims to provide a direct access emergency shelter for young people with allied outreach workers operating on the streets of Naples. This scheme involves collaboration between public services and local religious bodies.

During the last academic year just over 91,000 students were registered at the University of Naples and of these over 27,000 lived in the city. The main student welfare organisation, the Opera, received 234 applications for accommodation in the year 1986/87 in comparison with approximately 180 beds at its disposal. This exceptionally low level of demand is attributed to apathy and disillusionment among the students. In contrast the political wing of Cattolici Popolari, a militant catholic group, has established a co-operative which obtains large properties for rent to students at levels well below those charged on the open market.

As in Bologna a range of provision exists for young people who have been severely marginalised. Authorised private boarding schools provide accommodation for young people who might otherwise be sent to prison and there are small communities run by priests offering similar facilites. It is estimated that there are around 8,000 registered drug addicts in the city of Naples, many of whom are young people. In response there are only three reception centres for addicts in the city and six in the region as a whole. For unmarried mothers there are five places in two flats run by a priest while a religious order offers hospitality to a maximum of 18 young people discharged from Poggio Reale prison, where 80% of the inmates are under 30 years of age.

France

The most significant national level initiative is represented by the social security system which in France is run exclusively for the benefit of its actual contributors. Young people who have not entered working life therefore find themselves outside the system which provides insurance cover and social assistance simply because they have not had the opportunity to become contributors. However, there is a wide range of 'solidarity measures' operated by the national state, the departements and the communes. These measures include allowances for unemployed young people which will give them a guaranteed minimum income and assistance with rent payments.

The existence of many different allowances does not always ensure that the young people intended to receive them actually do so. In some cases young people are simply unaware of their entitlements whilst in others the bureaucratic procedures associated with paying an allowance are so complicated and slow that many claimants give up before receiving any money. Moreover, a number of the allowances - especially those concerned with accommodation - are only available to families of one sort or another. Because young people are less likely to be the head of any type of family unit they are less likely to be eligible for this type of assistance.

The main response to the problems faced by young leaving home in search of work in the post-war years was the construction of a national network of Young Workers' Hostels. From the early 1950s cheap finance was made available in the form of 45 year loans at 1% annual interest to build these hostels and over the next 20 years 470 were constructed to provide 45,000 rooms. Although access was limited originally to young people who were actually receiving wages this was relaxed in the 1970s. In the 1970s unemployment began to affect young people and the hostels developed programmes of vocational training and further education.

Nearly half of the Young Workers' Hostels are owned by the HLMs, a third belong to associations (both religious and others), whilst the remainder -amounting to around one in six belong to local government organisations or to private companies.

Hostels tend to attract residents from within their own region and indeed from the departement in which they are situated, but a significant minority of residents (13%) come from abroad. Nationally 48% of hostel residents have steady jobs and 15% are students. The remaining 37% are in a more insecure position with only temporary jobs, no job at all or on some form of apprenticeship scheme. Recently approximately 100,000 young people between 16 and 25 years of age have sought a hostel place each year. They include young people who leave home to start work, those who simply want to live independently of their parents and young people who might otherwise be placed in some form of institution. A survey carried out in 1981 found that young people from large families made up 75% of the population of Young Workers' Hostels, a fact which implies that large families are less able to support young members than others.

In 1971 another national policy response was made to the problems faced by young people in the form of giving them assistance with meeting their accommodation costs. Since 1985 this had required the young person to enter into a contract with the management of the hostels and is limited to a three month period.

Bauer and Cuzon describe young workers' hostels as "the hard core of services for the reception and shelter of disadvantaged young people in France". They also note that young people are increasingly turning away from the hostels, which rarely achieve an occupany rate of more than 80%. "The hostels are no longer in tune with the spirit of the times" but are performing an emergency accommodation to a growing extent.

Accommodation for unmarried mothers has been provided in a variety of forms since the turn of the century. Each departement was obliged to provide at least one maternity home and since the 1960s these have provided additional post-natal support services. Current policy aims to make special provision for only the most disadvantaged young women while trying to introduce the majority of young women to the mainstream public housing market. The total number of centres for unmarried mothers is not apparent but it appears that they are not subject to excessive demand at present.

Other national level organisations providing assistance to young people, among others, include the Salvation Army, Emmaus, Secours Catholique and ATD Quart Monde. In addition, FNARS - a national federation of associations providing accommodation and other social services - accounts for approximately 370 centres with a capacity of 15,000 beds which accommodate 80,000 people each year.

The local case studies were carried out in two areas that display both similarities and differences. Both areas contain a large population of manual workers and a relatively large proportion of immigrants. However, one of the areas chosen, the Lorraine region, is suffering the consequences of severe decline in the steel industry while the other, Lyon, has weathered the recession relatively well due to the size and diversity of its industrial base.

Bauer and Cuzon focused on two communes within the Lorraine region - Moyeuvre-Grande in Moselle and Neuves-Maisons in Meurthe-et-Moselle - as areas that suffered acutely under the crisis. In both areas new house building has virtually stopped and large numbers of property are now empty. In the face of this crisis the issue of young people's housing problems does not seem to have attracted a lot of political interest:

> The local politicians we met are far more worried about the economic crisis than by its social consequences. (Bauer and Cuzon, p 117).

The response of many young people, at least those who are able, is to leave Lorraine altogether or go to Nancy or Metz. In these two cities the housing problems faced by young people seem to receive much greater attention.

Although the city of Lyon does not face the same scale of problems as the towns and cities of the Lorraine region, it does contain pockets of poverty, especially on its eastern side. In this area there are some very large social housing complexes which were the scene a few years ago of demonstrations organised by young people of Maghrebine backgrounds. Apart from this example it is suggested that accommodation for young people is not a source of social tension nor is it leading to political demands being made on the local housing institutions. Bauer and Cuzon do, however, suggest that detailed information about the housing situation of young people at a local level is very patchy and that this often leads to inappropriate policy responses:

> .... on the one hand there is a methodological and theoretical inability to seize the totality of this social phenomena; while on the other hand the individual social situations .... provide images of society which are tangible and attractive but they tend to confuse the individual case with the general experience. (p 136)

The Lorraine regional authority has not included social action in its priority objectives but has passed its responsibilities down to the level of the departements. The social service functions of the departements support young workers' hostels and shelter centres but their intervention is based on an insecure financial regime which renders them liable to withdraw at any time.

At the grassroots level the Commune's Social Action Centre (CCAS) provide emergency assistance and short term reception, while young unmarried mothers are able to benefit from the nationally determined isolated parent allowances (API). Young people with few financial assets and poor employment prospects are finding it increasingly difficult to obtain HLM properties as these organisations are taking a tougher financial line with prospective tenants.

Four other initiatives are worth noting:

'Le Grand Sauvoy", an Association of young workers' hostels in Maxeville, a commune on the outskirts of Nancy. This has recently focused its attention on young men aged between 16 and 25 who have no jobs and little training. The Association offers shelter and gives individual advice and support in moving towards independent living. Four units operate including an emergency reception centre, a lodging centre with 130 places, a training centre offering workshop courses and a young workers' hostel. Staff working for the Association have a pessimistic view of the future because of the increasing level of 'social maladjustment' of young people using their facility and the ever increasing demands of potential employers.

The Carrefour Hostel in Metz. This is a non-profit association which aims to provide young women with accommodation, meals and a programme of educational and social development. In 1982 a mutual housing association was established to improve the housing opportunities available to young people by liaising with public authorities and other housing providers. The association can advance loans to young people, arrange insurance schemes and provide general help in checking leases, carrying surveys of properties and so on. The hostel also runs a centre to help young people adjust to working life in which training courses are provided. This programme is reserved for young women aged between 16 and 25 and caters for a substantial number (over 40%) of young women of 'foreign origin'.

The Moselle association for information and mutual aid (AIEM) in Metz. This consists of a lodging centre, a mutual housing association (AMUL) and a social/education programme (ASEL). AMUL brings together representatives of the departement, a national housing confederation, the Carrefour and a psychotherapy centre. It caters for any individual or family in difficulty on a non-selective basis. One quarter of those helped are under 25 years of age though and 60% are young single women.

The final initiative is Centr'aide Moselle. While this is only a small scale initiative it is worthy of mention because it was established by a State agency - Moselle DDASS - in response to the number of young people looking for emergency shelter in the winter of 1985/86. 50 young people have been taken in since the centre opened and they have typically had no resources whatsoever.

The urban area of Lyon has managed to stay in reasonably good economic health over recent years and its unemployment rate if currently two percentage points below the national average. This overall picture masks some significant pockets of poverty though, especially on the eastern edges of the city. We discuss some of these patterns of difference more fully in the next chapter.

Within the centre of Courly, the Lyon urban area, very few young people who are heads of households are tenants within the HLM sector. This is explained by the reduced supply of HLM accommodation and by the easy access to pre-1948 properties at low rents. The older quarters of Lyon therefore contain a relatively high proportion of young people who tend to be highly mobile.

The groups of young people most susceptible to housing problems include, unsurprisingly, those labelled as marginalised and those young people newly arrived in the city. The two main responses to the problems faced by these groups are shelter centres and young workers' hostels. Shelter centres total 30 in the Lyon area and take in approximately 3,000 people every year. Young people under the age of 21 represent less than one fifth of this total although 'non French' people account for almost one third. The type of problems presented by these groups and the details of the responses made are said not to vary according to the age of the 'client'. Nevertheless, a major problem is seen to be the accommodation problems of young people leaving the shelter centres especially those who face discrimination because they are 'foreigners', because they are young or handicapped or because they have been in prison.

Young workers' hostels provide accommodation for young people and include those affiliated to the national union and independent hostels. The latter are frequently in serious financial difficulties and those which cater specifically for immigrants (the Sonacotra hostels for example) do not tend to house many young people. Many mutual housing associations have been set up by the hostels in order to help young people but at present they have not managed to play an effective co-ordinating role between all the relevant agencies. The director of one association said:

> .... the young people's mutual housing association has not yet reached its cruising speed; it is merely ticking over .... we have not succeeded in our attempt at positioning ourselves at city level. (Quoted in Bauer and Cuzon, p 152.)

Finally, it is useful to bear in mind that young people have responded to the limitations of their housing circumstances in novel ways. For example, it is reported that young people in Lyon are highly mobile to the extent that they may spend part of the week living with their parents in one part of town and spend the weekends with friends who have apartments in the city centre:

> This residential mobility, connected with the circulation of young people in the conurbation in search of work, or to go to the same places of leisure, makes one think that for certain age-bands residential mobility is a formula allowing them to test various possibilities and find the best one. (Bauer and Cuzon, p 154)

The Netherlands

As Deelstra and Schokkenbroek (1988) point out in their report, housing for young people is attracting a great deal of interest in the Netherlands at present. At the national level the Ministry of Housing, Physical Planning and the Environment commissioned a study on housing needs and 'supervised lodging' projects are currently being evaluated. These projects are for people with serious psychiatric problems or physical handicaps and are the responsibility of a National Foundation. National groups representing the interests of young people have also been active, for example the National Organisation of Housing Interest Groups held a symposium on the future of housing for young people in the spring of 1988. At the same time there are indications that the housing opportunities available to young people are diminishing in the face of urban redevelopment schemes, rising rents and the impact of youth unemployment. It is against this background that we look at responses made to the housing problems of young people in the Netherlands.

Until 1970 young people were ignored when calculations were made of the future demand for housing. Unsurprisingly most construction was geared towards the needs of conventional family units and most dwellings were built with four or five rooms. Rented rooms, on which the majority of young people relied for their accommodation if they were not living with their parents, declined dramatically as a proportion of the total stock. In 1970 though a policy document was prepared by the Secretary of State for Housing which responded to the needs of one and two person households by subsidising the construction of small, low rent dwellings. These are known as HAT dwellings and over 77,000 had been built by 1985. Half of all the tenants of HAT properties are single people under the age of 25. In many cases, however, young people's access to these properties was restricted by residency clauses applied by the municipality.

Room letting is another common form of accommodation for young people, whether it is in properties owned by a private landlord or by housing associations or municipalities - a practice known as 'social room letting'. Although many rooms let in this way are very small the rents charged are often high. At the same time some fiscal measures make it relatively unattractive for property owners to let spare rooms to young people because of punitive rental taxes. Slightly more than half of all lodgers spend over 30% of their income on living expenses.

From the early 1960s student housing complexes were built in the university cities because of considerable demand from students. In 1986 the Student Housing Associations managed a total of 40,000 units which are now (except in Tilburg) open to all young people. A recent survey found that over 16,000 people were currently on the waiting lists of all the associations (quoted in Deelstra and Schokkenbroek, p 75).

Communal living is also popular in the Netherlands although a Study on Housing Needs carried out in 1981 estimated that only 0.2% of all people aged 18 - 24 lived in this way. Other research carried out in Rotterdam estimated that 37,000 people lived in communes and half of them were under 25 years of age. While the number can be disputed it is clear that the vast majority of communes exist in rented properties and that these are among the most unsuitable types of property for this style of living.

Squatting - in other words occupying an empty property without the consent of the owner - has a long tradition in the Netherlands. Attention was focused on squatting in the early 1980s because of street battles with the authorities, most noticeably in Amsterdam and Nijmegen. A ministerial working party was set up in 1983 to study this phenomenon in Leiden, The Hague, Groningen and Breda and estimated the number of squatters in these areas as almost 4,500. Most squatters are young people who want to solve their own housing problems in ways that suit their own needs rather than those of someone else. It is suggested that young black people in the Netherlands do not resort to squatting to the same extent as young whites because it may jeopardise their chances of securing residence permits. The majority of squatted properties - including offices, industrial buildings and churches - have been empty for at least six months prior to their occupation and in this sense they represent an addition to the housing stock. This line of argument does not, however, appear to have impressed the state as legislation was introduced in 1987 to limit the rights of 'illegal' occupants of vacant buildings.

The National Foundation for the Care and Shelter of the Homeless exists to provide shelter, care and counselling for single people aged 18 and over who typically have been involved in crime. The Foundation runs eight shelters that offer facilities to 140 people but the proportion of young people (under 20 years) is very small. Other hostels provide a similar service but have more places (approximately 1,600) and cater for a slightly higher proportion of young people. The Ministry of Housing, Physical Planning and the Environment estimate that up to 10,500 'independent units' and up to 13,000 'supervised units' are required to meet the needs of the people who currently rely on hostels of one sort or another. There is some provision nationally of supervised living units, where young people who are almost able to cope with independent living can be housed and supported. The requirements imposed by this type of institution - no serious mental health problems, nobody with a serious drug addiction problem, some income etc - exclude most young people who might be described as 'marginalised'.

We conclude by quoting Deelstra and Schokkenbroek:

> At the moment there is no specific policy on housing for young people .... Yet there is a great demand for accommodation among young people, and they are taking all kinds of new initiatives, including the establishment of communes and places where they can combine living, working and cultural activities. Sadly these solutions are confined to the fringes of the housing sector and the relationship between effort and effect is so unreasonable as not to really alleviate the situation in the housing market. (p 93)

We now describe briefly some initiatives taken throughout the Netherlands to improve the housing conditions of young people, before looking more closely at the situation in Amsterdam.

Two projects run by and for young women in Nijmegen are particularly noteworthy. The first is a house where 13 women, all around the age of 25, live and work. The house was built as a school and is being renovated at present. It houses a bicycle workshop, the editorial team of a women's newspaper and a screen printing shop. The women now want to restore the property extensively but the municipality plans to demolish it. We do not know of their decision yet. In the same town the 'Hysterica' foundation runs a hostel for up to six women who have been in psychiatric institutions. There is intensive support provided and most of the residents, who stay for up to three months, move on to a supervised living project or commune. The foundation relies on subsidies however and if public health care resources continue to be cut then the hostel may have to close.

In the Hague young immigrants who are forced to leave home can turn to the Casa Migrantes supervised living project. This has been in existence for five years now and receives support from the municipality. The project attempts to reconcile the young people with their families or relatives in the first instance but if this fails then they are housed independently. Three properties are currently available with a total of 26 places and a separate counselling centre is planned. The Casa Migrantes Foundation is planning to broaden its activities now to include emergency reception, peripatetic counselling and training in independent living.

The Transvaal district of the Hague is a neighbourhood with a very high population density and a large proportion of young people, many of whom are the children of immigrants. In 1982 a project was established to deal with two related problems - unemployment and lack of housing opportunities for young people. It aims to allow young people to restore empty and derelict properties which they will then be able to live in and also to receive training in construction sector skills. The young workers also carry out small scale repair work for other local people who are otherwise unable to afford to maintain their homes. An agreement was reached with local squatter groups not to occupy properties that were earmarked for renovation. The formal construction of this project means that the participants are eligible for a range of state allowances such as removal expenses and rent subsidies. The project has therefore become the focus for a wide range of activities for young people from the area but it is threatened now by the lack of suitable properties as more conventional forms of urban renewal take place.

Throughout the Netherlands empty premises have been squatted by young people seeking to combine living, working and cultural activities under one roof. In Wageningen, for example, four young people established a restaurant in a derelict workshop in which they were living, while in Ubbergen an old monastery was restored and now houses 79 people aged from three to almost 80, although most are in their 20s. In Groningen a disused hospital was taken over by squatters and now houses 250 people in a building which also contains workshops, a cinema, a disco and a restaurant. Most of the residents are in their early 20s. The Port Building in Rotterdam was abandoned in 1978 and squatted by 30 young people in 1980 as a protest against the opening of an official brothel and the local housing shortage. The residents have now formed a collective association which organises the housekeeping, maintenance and further conversion work.

Amsterdam was chosen as the main case study area for a number of reasons - it contains all the different types of neighbourhood which are found in Dutch cities in general, including areas of decline as well as areas of relative prosperity; it plays something of a pioneering role in the cultural sphere in particular and it acts as a centre for socially innovatory movements for young people. We start by describing some interesting responses to the problems of homelessness (in its widest sense) in Amsterdam, before moving on to examine in more detail the situation in three contrasting localities within the city.

In the spring of 1987 a workshop was held in Amsterdam with the title 'Control over your own home'. It was attended by young people from all over the country with an interest in combined living and working projects and organised by two squatters' associations from the city and a non-commercial accommodation agency - SIKH. The workshop was held in the former Wilhelmina Hospital which is now run by the group WG-terrein and the participants saw a range of initiatives and activities organised by groups from all over the city. The non-commercial accommodation agency SIKH is itself worthy of note as it represents a response from a national trade union body to the housing problems faced by young people. Originally set up to cater for students it now offers a service to all young people under 30 by providing agency services, helping young people to register with housing associations and acting as a mediator for squatter groups. Young people are also represented on the board of management of SIKH.

The squatter movement in Amsterdam was represented in print by the weekly paper 'Bluf!' which covered issues of urban politics and housing problems and was read by thousands of people throughout the country. Bluf! ceased publication in the spring of 1988. In a similar vein SPOK, the Speculation Research Collective focuses attention on speculative house owners and the increasing gentrification of central Amsterdam and published its findings in a series of black books. The National Organisation of Housing Interest Groups is a more conventional research body which has investigated many aspects of housing throughout the Netherlands. The Amsterdam section is particularly active and last year (1987) held symposia on urban renewal, the re-use of buildings and state subsidy systems.

Three areas of Amsterdam illustrate the diversity of problems faced by young people looking for decent accommodation and the responses that have developed. These areas are the Indian Quarter, the Bijlmermeer and the Ij Island.

The Indian Quarter is a typical working class district with a high level of unemployment at present. Many of the houses in the Quarter are of poor quality although recently some newly built housing has attracted a more prosperous group of people into the area. Social tensions are quite high as these different groups are forced to co-exist and this is exacerbated by racism and other forms of racial hostility between the different groups who live in the area. About one third of the young people who live in the area are of foreign origin, most coming from Surinam, Turkey and Morocco. A survival strategy adopted by many of these young people has been to form street gangs although membership often leads to criminalisation. In response to these problems the parents of some young drug addicts formed an organisation, known as SHID, to help their children. SHID employs a team of social workers and doctors as well as detached community workers and operates from a centre in the Quarter. It organises a wide range of activities including sports, drop in facilities and summer projects.

SHID argues that at present policy for young people - covering health, social affairs, education, housing and employemnt - is fragmented and this makes it diffucult to develop a comprehensive and coherent service. They also feel that this is increasingly important as the housing situation of young people deteriorates. In particular, they see the trend towards higher rents and lower benefits creating a new nomadic class among young people. SHID itself, dependent on municipal and government subsidy, is not optimistic about its own survival and fears that it, along with many young people, will simply disappear from public view.

The Bijlmermeer was the last major project to extend the city of Amsterdam to the south. It was designed in the 1960s and mostly built in the early 1970s in the modern style of architecture. Workplaces were deliberately kept away from the area and shops and other social facilities were not built until the houses were occupied. After Surinam gained its independence from the Netherlands a significant number of immigrants settled in the Bijlmermeer along with smaller number of Turks and Morrocans. Among the Surinamese young people there are two distinct groups - those who came with their parents in the 1970s and those born here in subsequent years. The former have always experienced high levels of unemployment and have tended to become very marginalised while the latter, younger groups have embraced the values of Dutch society more wholeheartedly and are more integrated.

One initiative of note was taken by a group of five older Surinamese women on behalf of younger girls who had a pronounced tendency to get pregnant as a means of achieving short-term housing benefits and obtaining a degree of social status within their community. The five women organised a musical in which the younger girls took part and in the year which it took to plan and prepare for the production none of them became pregnant. The project demonstrated to the municipal authorities, who eventually offered some financial support, that preventative work was far more effective than offering support after an event.

The final illustrative locality within the city of Amsterdam is the Ij Island. This was originally the major port area of the city, but it became redundant when activity shifted to the west. The old port buildings have been squatted since 1980 and house approximately 500 mainly young people. In addition, a number of people live in houseboats moored in the old dock areas and the Greenpeace boat Sirius is berthed in one quay. Many old spaces are now put to imaginative use. For example, a circus keeps its animals in some empty sheds during the winter, an empty cattle market is now a caravan park, there are some 50 different workshops and two restaurant/cafes primarily for the residents. The vast majority of the young residents are of Dutch origin and few ethnic minority groups live on the Island.

In 1978 the municipal authorities decided to change the use of the whole area and in the mid-1980s revealed plans to create a new residential area combining social and private housing. The growing requirements of profitability have reduced the scope for low cost housing elements and, in addition, the planners found it difficult to accommodate the aspirations of the young residents. These have developed through a series of meetings and the establishment of a residents' group which has now published a Memorandum of Principles governing the future development of the Island. They include slow pace of change so that the social and physical environment can evolve organically and a commitment to 'alternative' energy sources.

The local authority has decided that it will not accept the proposals of the residents of the Ij island. The young people who have made the Island their home cannot therefore look to the future with any certainty.

Federal Republic of Germany

The overall balance of the housing stock in the Federal Republic is not suited to the needs of young, mainly single people as more than half of it consists of three and four room units. While 32% of households consist of one person, only 11% of all units are one or two roomed. Likewise the bulk of new stock built since the 1970s had not suited young people as it has typically been for owner-occupation. Publicly-funded housebuilding programmes have been cut back increasingly as more state assistance has been directed at owner-occupiers. Because home purchase in the Federal Republic usually takes place at a relatively late age - ie between the ages of 40 and 50 - the measures which support it do not apply to young people at all. Young people, along with the low-paid, the unemployed and foreigners have also lost out in recent years as the more wealthy sections of German society have begun to move back into the centre of cities and to price the former occupants out of the local housing market.

The local case studies were selected on the basis of a distinction between the 'north' and the 'south' of the country. While acknowledging the differences that obviously exist within these regions there is a growing recognition of the ever widening gap between the prosperous south and the depressed north. This is reflected to some extent in a greater housing shortage in the south as it is an area of in-migration whereas the north has been losing population. Jablonka et al expected the standard of housing, as measured by the existence of basic amenities, to be higher in the south in line with higher rental levels. Taking all these factors into account the major housing problems in the north are associated with the standard of amenities and the condition of the housing stock, while in the south the main problem is an absolute shortage of housing.

Hamburg and Stuttgart in Baden-Wurttemburg were chosen to reflect, respectively, these north/south differences. Hamburg is affected by structural weaknesses in its economy while Stuttgart is benefiting from above average growth rates in its motor vehicle and high-tech industries. The overall unemployment rates, as well as those for young people, are above the national average in Hamburg and below in Stuttgart while figures for the construction of public sector houses show the same pattern. In terms of policy responses to the housing problems faced by young people, in Stuttgart the main emphasis in on welfare initiatives, while in Hamburg it is on urban renewal schemes. It is not clear, however, whether this reflects the different economic circumstances of each area described above.

In Hamburg the Schroderstift Tenants' Co-operative was formed as a self-help project to repair and then manage a redundant old people's home that was threatened with demolition. The building had been bought by the city of Hamburg to accommodate the expansion of the University, but these plans were dropped in the mid 1970s. The students began to organise themselves and to demand first improvements in the communal facilities of the building and then its complete rehabilitation. The Co-operative was formed in the early 1980s and renovation plans produced which eventually received support from the local authority in the form of grant in 1981. The residents of the building all participated in its renovation, although additional skilled workers were also engaged - they did however provide training for the unskilled members of the group.

The renovation work did not affect the size of the flats nor the overall number available and rents are now set at a level which is low for the city. To some extent the resident population has aged, although a number have now moved on to more appropriate accommodation, the average age of tenants is now between 25 and 35. The Co-operative has gone on to found another non-profit making society to renovate another building which will cater for young people. It is financed by the City of Hamburg Department of Labour, Youth and Social Welfare and other organisations including a church group.

The second initiative is an "alternative urban renewal organisation". This is based on models which originated in Berlin in the conflicts over urban redevelopment schemes. In Hamburg there was increasing opposition to the destruction of reasonably priced accommodation and the displacement of the traditional inhabitants of the city centre, and in 1981 the local authority approved a budget for an 'old buildings renovation scheme for the maintenance of a cheap housing stock'. Since 1987 the city of Hamburg has officially recognised two such alternative redevelopment organisations - the Stattbau Hamburg and the Johann-Daniel-Lawaetz-Stiftung. The latter was etablished by the local authorities while the Stattbau comprises three local action groups. Both organisations aim to help groups of local people participate in the renovation of properties, giving them somewhere to live and the chance to develop their skills in the process. Although it is not necessarily so, in practice young people have been most interested in participating in these schemes. One of the biggest problems faced by these organisations has been the high expectations held by local politicians and other participants. This has put the schemes under a lot of pressure and made it difficult to cope with the problems and delays which frequently beset any building programme.

Two schemes supported by Stattbau illustrate the possibilities of this initiative. The Inner City Altona Self-help Association was formed in 1983, ostensibly to organise a fire protection scheme for a large empty building. The group then developed proposals for the renovation of the building which is now almost complete. The small flats of the original building have now been converted into larger units which can house groups of five or six people. Twenty people now live in the building, most of them aged between 20 and 30 years and they have a high level of commitment to achieving their housing objectives and to expanding their political consciousness.

The second scheme is an Association for the Retention of Historical and Public Housing, located in St. Pauli. A row of historical buildings were faced with demolition until the Independent Youth Workshops Association advocated their preservation and were supported by the city authorities. In association with Stattbau, plans were drawn up the for renovation of the buildings which should be complete in the near future. Accommodation will be available for 12 young people who must have been involved in the training workshops run by the Association.

In 1979 the Protestant Church in co-operation with the local Social Assistance Department established a counselling centre for young people 'with especially serious social problems'. The centre provides counselling help with finding accommodation and a job and help with education and making social contacts. Although young people as a group had not been regarded as a group at risk, workers reported that over the last few years the danger of them losing their accommodation had grown. Therefore, separate provision was made to offer counselling and other facilities specifically for young peole with no accommodation. For legal reasons the service is limited to German and Austrian nationals, although young foreigners are in practice not denied access. It is worth noting that there is only one other facility like this in the rest of the Federal Republic.

The centre employs four workers whose responsibilities are to provide counselling, to help in finding accommodation, to ensure that young people receive their proper entitlement under the state welfare programmes and to help them in searching for a job or training place. The workers rely on a number of different sources for accommodating young people. The two main religious denominations run hostels for young people, although these are at present overcrowded and workers are forced to use a home for men of all ages, which is not considered especially suitable for young people. The centre itself has four flats with a total of 16 places, but there is little turnover of residents and places seldom become free. In some limited cases a hotel room can be found, especially for a bridging period and the centre can arrange for clients to obtain, from the Social Assistance Department, accommodation vouchers that can be 'cashed' at local estate agents. In 1986 the centre helped 453 peope of which 364 were young men and 89 young women.

A growing feature of youth work in Stuttgart has been dealing with housing problems faced by young people, in particular the need for emergency accommodation. Jablonka et al describe three youth work centres - the Society for Youth Fieldwork in Stuttgart/Frieberg/Monchfeld/Rot and the Association of Social Youth Work in Stuttgart East. We shall concentrate here only on the Hallschlag centre. This has some emergency accommodation available to young people attending the centre based on the principle that it is important to be able to offer accommodation in the part of town from which the young person comes in order that they can maintain their contacts and social networks. While the accommodation is provided for a period of four weeks, there is the possibility of renewal and the policy is not adhered to strictly. The occupants enter into a social contract concerning the payment of rent and other matters including receiving visitors and allowing access to staff of the scheme.

The Society for Youth Fieldwork has also developed another model for accommodating young people. Some young people who attend the centre are given the role of 'lay counsellors' when they take on certain voluntary tasks. An agreement has been reached with the local authority housing construction company to allocate some properties to these lay counsellors. This is quite unique as vacant accommodation is usually given to families. As Jablonka et al point out, 'the lay counsellors are thereby given the opportunity of living in the area to which they are committed .... (which is) .... also said to have a positive impact on social cohesion in the district which is somewhat run down'.

The final initiative to describe is known as the 'New Life in Old Walls' Association. In 1982 a group of young adults organised themselves to provide a combined living and working environment in a disused factory in an old part of Stuttgart. Their main aims were to provide themselves with cheap accommodation and to retain a high degree of self-determination over its use and management, to break down the distinctions between living and working space and to integrate themselves with the local neighbourhood.

The group comprised people with vocational qualifications, students and university graduates - in other words a relatively highly educated group - and they formed an incorporated association rather than a co-operative society, as this required very few formalities. They faced a number of legal and administrative difficulties, not least in putting together a viable financial package and indeed all the members took significant financial risks in supporting the scheme. The group has now founded a second society (Sudkultur) which is recongnised as a 'public benefit organisation' and which leases out a pub and rents out a large room for social events.

The housing units do not conform to traditional designs for living - preference is given to common space rather than private area and glass panels are used extensively to partition rooms. Most of the building work, apart from some specialist tasks, was carried out by the group members themselves who were paid a nominal rate of DM 10.00 per hour which was then counted as a capital resource.

The positive lessons to be learnt from this initiative are now being analysed by the Sudkultur Society with the support of a grant from the Labour Exchange. This should enable similar groups in the area to realise their own ambitions more effectively.

England

Three case study localities were chosen in England in order to illustrate some of the factors which structure young people's housing opportunities, and a series of responses from each area are described below. First, however, we examine some of the responses developed at the national level in relation to labour market measures, housing policies, area-based initiatives and social welfare provisions.

Mainly under the auspices of the Manpower Services Commission (now the Training Commission) a number of training and labour market policies have been directed at young people. An important element of most of these policy measures - from the Youth Opportunities Programme, through the Youth Training Scheme to the Young Workers Scheme - has been an attempt to lower the wage expectations of young people when they enter the labour market. Allowances and wage levels have been depressed in order that young people will 'price themselves back into jobs'. While this has taken place to some extent it has meant that young workers frequently do not earn enough to enable them to live away from their parents.

On the housing front the Housing (Homeless Persons) Act of 1977 gave limited rights to housing to various categories of homeless people. However, the limitations imposed in order to contain the effective demand for housing under this measure serve to exclude many young people. Applicants are classified according to priorities which favour those with dependent children and moreover they are excluded if they are deemed to have made themselves homeless, if they are not vulnerable or if they do not have any local connections. Current national government housing policies seek to extend home ownership, make the private rented sector more profitable and reduce the role of local authorities as landlords. There is little specific attention paid to homeless people in general or to the needs of young people seeking to live independently.

Area-based urban policies such as the Government's Urban Programme and other elements of the 'Action for Cities' initiative have some impact on the opportunities available to young people. The young unemployed have been a target group under the Urban Programme for some years and housing schemes have been supported. It must be pointed out, though, that in most of the local authorities where resources have been provided under these schemes, substantially greater cuts have been made in existing budgets which might in the past have helped young people.

Finally, in relation to the system of social security and welfare recent policy measures have tended to restrict young people's abilities to live independently. For example, since 1985 single people under the age of 26 have had time limits placed on their entitlement to claim benefits for accommodation costs. This has meant that young people have been forced to move frequently in order to maintain their entitlement and a roof over their head. As a national welfare rights campaigning group has put it, the British social security system was not designed to cope with large numbers of long-term unemployed people.

> .... still less was it ever expected to provide the means whereby young people made the transition from childhood to adulthood'.
> (quoted in Burton, Forrest and Stewart, 1987, p 28.)

Three areas were chosen for limited case study work - the north east, the south west and London. The north east is an area that has suffered dramatically as a result of the last recession but has a much longer history of economic decline. Unemployment rates throughout the region are higher than the national average and in some areas unemployment affects virtually every household. The mortality rate is high as are rates of illegitimate birth and the proportion of children in the care of the local authority. The last figure is important as it has a very strong association with homelessness among young people in their late teens. Levels of owner occupation are very low while a very high proportion of the population live in social rented housing.

The south west is relative prosperous and has weathered the recession better than many other regions of the country. The housing stock has been increasing over the last decade and levels of owner occupation are high. Bristol is the regional capital and has succeeded in restructuring its economy without unemployment rising rapidly. There are pockets where unemployment is very high and registered unemployment has reached record levels. In the third local case study area, London, there is now an absolute shortage of housing and a large proportion of the stock is poor condition. The cost of housing in relation to average income levels is high and has risen rapidly in recent years as house price inflation has taken off. There is very little new building of social housing, especially in the inner London boroughs and waiting lists have grown substantially as new households form. Although the London case is exceptional rather than typical it cannot be ignored because so many young people continue to migrate there from the rest of the country (and abroad) in search of work, housing and an exciting life style. In this sense it is more directly comparable with the other capital cities described in the national case studies, eg Athens, Amsterdam, Lisbon and Dublin.

In the north east of England, in Newcastle, the Bridges Project has been providing resources for young people and others working on behalf of young people in the fields of addictions, health, civil liberties and housing. The housing work they have supported includes convening meetings of local housing workers, campaigning for better provision from the local authority and producing a video which demonstrates the problems faced by young people leaving care. Another project, more concerned with direct provision, is called Stepping Stones and offers short term emergency accommodation to young people who are homeless. The project has received funds from two national policy initiatives, the Urban Programme and the Community Programme, to cover capital and revenue costs. In the year to March 1986, 85 young people were housed by Stepping Stones out of 461 young people who applied. Most were turned down simply because there were no spaces available but a small minority (2%) were considered unsuitable because of their behaviour or attitudes.

To the south of Newcastle in Middlesbrough, the local authority decided to respond to the growing demand for housing from young single people by converting two blocks of family flats into accommodation more suited to the needs of this group. Communal facilities were installed and the existing flats were converted into apartments for groups of single sharers. Some of the day-to-day management problems created as a result of large groups of young people living in close proximity for the first time were solved by the employment of support workers. These workers provide welfare rights advice and have also succeeded in involving the young people in the management of the buildings.

Two projects in Bristol in the south west are especially noteworthy. The first was initiated by a local magistrate in the wake of uprisings on the streets of the St. Paul's district in the early 1980s. The intention was to help a group of young people build their own homes and acquire some skills in the process that would help them to get jobs. The Zenzele Self Build Housing Association was therefore formed in 1983 by twelve young men, eleven of whom were black. Some were unemployed at the time and all were experiencing unsatisfactory living conditions. With the support of a range of local people the group completed the construction of a block of 12 flats in 1985 and four of them went on to form their own construction company.

Also in the centre of Bristol is the Brighton Street Hostel which offers emergency accommodation to young women who need a relatively high level of support. The hostel has been in operation since 1970 and can house up to eight young women with the support of five staff. A Community Support Service also runs from the hostel and past residents are encouraged to drop in during the day if they need longer term support. Apart from an overall lack of resources, project workers have expressed concern about having to turn away young women with severe emotional or behavioural problems.

A recent research report on homelessness in London identified a number of important characteristics of the London housing market. There is now an absolute shortage of housing and a large proportion of the stock is in poor condition; the cost of housing relative to income levels is very high and rising; a wide range of individuals and households are at risk of becoming homeless and there is extensive racial and gender discrimination in all sectors of the housing market. There are a great many projects and initiatives responding to the needs of young people who are homeless or roofless or who face problems obtaining decent housing, and we describe two below to illustrate something of the diversity.

In Lewisham, an area of South London, a housing project called Stopover offers accommodation to homeless young people at two hostels. One provides emergency accommodation for up to nine young people who can refer themselves as well as being referred by other agencies. Residents stay for up to four weeks during which time they are helped in clarifying their housing needs and working out how to meet them. At the other hostel young people can stay for up to one year and are supported by five full time workers who provide 24 hour a day cover. The intention is to provide a stable and secure environment in which the young residents can acquire the skills that will enable them to live independently.

The project is presently facing an uncertain future as one of its sponsors, the Greater London Council, has now been abolished while the other, the London Borough of Lewisham has suffered substantial financial penalties and may not be able to continue its support.

The other initiative is an umbrella group for a variety of housing and youth organisations. The Young Homelessness Group was formed in 1982:

> to promote, locally and nationally, a greater understanding of the distinctive needs of young people - particularly their need for adequate accommodation and income, sympathetic housing management, good information and education about housing - and to press for these needs to be met. (Burton, Forrest and Stewart, p 45).

The group produces reports on various aspects of housing for young people as well as briefing papers when new legislation is introduced. Other resources such as exhibitions and slide shows have also been distributed as part of campaigns to improve the situation for young people.

Ireland

Almost half the population of Ireland is aged under 25 and approximately 18% are aged between 15 and 25. This has meant that the social and economic needs of young people have been given particular attention by the government. A National Youth Policy Committee was formed in the early 1980s which spelt out its views in a discussion paper in 1983:

> We have a unique situation now in Irish society with about half our population under the age of 25. This alone will compel us to attend to fundamental issues and problems in our social, political and economic system. But there are other equally important reasons why everybody should be involved in an examination of policy affecting youth - chief among these is that our young people will create and shape the future of our society well into the middle of the next century. (Quoted in Ronayne, 1987, p 2).

The same committee has also noted the need to develop policies for young people in order to avoid the rapid growth of a two class society, with the deprived underclass typically inhabiting the peripheral areas around the major towns and cities. (Ronayne, p 5).

Our case study has focused on Dublin, mainly because it houses over 30% of all young people in the country. These young residents are typically facing a bleak future as the supply of jobs that do not require high levels of qualifications and skill have been diminishing steadily, and unemployment has risen rapidly. When these trends are overlain with developments in housing policy we can see how young people are likely to lose out. Since the early 1970s Irish housing policy has been dominated by the demands of owner occupiers - to the same extent as the domination in the 1960s by working class local authority tenants. The sale of council houses and cuts in new building have reduced the stock of social housing to the detriment of young people (couples) in particular.

Dublin Corporation has, however, made some response to the housing needs of young people by making available 'difficult to let' properties vacated by families under a scheme, which subsidises households who surrender their council houses. The Ballymun area of Dublin has seen a significant increase in the number of single people and single parents housed, to the extent that local groups are now opposing the segregation and strain on local services that this has caused.

Housing associations and building co-operatives have traditionally played only a small part in Irish housing provision. They are, however, now beginning to provide for the needs of the elderly, homeless young mothers and young couples. (Ronayne p 56). It has been suggested that new government measures which subsidise social housing construction are most appropriate for well established voluntary sector groups with some capacity for funding, rather than smaller self-help groups with a lower public profile.

Finally we describe, briefly, a number of the responses to young people's housing problems that have developed in Dublin in recent years. In 1984 a new agency, Focus Point, was created to campaign around the issues of homelessness and to help people who are out-of-home to create a home of their own. This initiative emerged out of some research carried out by Sr Stanislaus Kennedy in 1983, which examined homelessness amongst young women in Dublin. Focus Point provides a meeting place in the centre of Dublin, an information service, a creative activities centre and an outreach team. The group also carries out research and can provide short term accommodation in an emergency.

It is worth quoting in full what Focus Point say about the terminology of homelessness:

> The stigmatism which is attached to the word 'homeless' is strongly demonstrated by the fact that those who are actually without a home of their own do not describe themselves as 'homeless'. People describe their situation in other ways: "I have nowhere to stay tonight", "I'm stuck for a while", "I'm in a squat" "I can't go back home". In recognition of this,.... (we) .... will not collectively describe people who are 'out of a home' as 'homeless'. When we use the term 'homeless' it is only to describe the state of being out of home. (Focus Point's First Report, 1987, p 4).

The Simon Community is a voluntary organisation working with homeless people in Britain as well as in Ireland. It runs four communities throughout Ireland in Cork, Dundalk, Galway and Dublin and has been in existence for almost twenty years. The Simon approach is based on four principles: developing a sense of community within its projects; accepting people as they are not as they ought to be; providing long-term care where necessary and campaigning for changes to government policy. The projects are on average 85% self-financing, with the remainder coming from the state. The majority of residents and others helped by the Projects are middle aged and male, but workers report that a growing number of the homeless with whom they work are young people.

At a national level in March 1984 a group of representatives from voluntary organisations concerned with homelessness formed the National Campaign for the Homeless. The Campaign elects an executive committee each year and organises its work through sub-committees on housing policy, young people and homelessness and European work.

Greece

As Emmanuel (p 1) points out:

> .... the concept of housing problems of the young as a distinct category of special problems is unfamiliar in the Greek context.

It would typically be taken as referring to the problems associated with teenagers or students living at home or to the problems faced by young couples. Some of the more extreme manifestations of homelessness among young people in other European countries, rooflessness for example, appear to be absent in Greece.

Leaving home and forming an independent household is associated almost entirely with marriage and there is little evidence of single person households or unmarried non-family households. The only significant exception to this is the case of students where there is widespread acceptance of the fact that they tend to live in non-family households. While it is estimated that approximately 60% of Greek students live away from their parents' home there is virtually no provision of any form of subsidised accommodation. The Student Housing Authority offers a total of 5,500 beds throughout the whole country, corresponding to less than 6% of the student population. The majority of students live in privately rented accommodation which is relatively expensive, reflecting the fact that the majority of higher degree students come from middle class backgrounds.

These observations largely explain why there are so few responses or initiatives directed at young people and their housing problems in Greece, especially when compared with other European countries. Social housing represents a small proportion of the total housing stock and new building in this sector has been carried out almost exclusively by the Workers' Housing Association. All the stock in this sector is intended for owner-occupation - there are no programmes for public rental housing. When the age profile of owner-occupiers is taken into account we see that it is not until people reach their mid-thirties that they begin to consider buying a home of their own. Thus young people rely almost totally on the private rented sector.

The only exception of note is a programme introduced in the early 1980s to help young couples to secure Workers' Housing but this suffers from chronic under-funding and has had a very limited impact. Two other schemes provide loans to young professional households but these are primarily regional relocation programmes rather than measures to help the young as such.

While there are few initiatives to describe it is possible to relate the following prognosis. Given young people's reliance on the private rented sector any significant reduction in its scope would be catastrophic for them. The imposition and relaxation of rent controls in recent years have given some indication of the sensitivity of the market and it is suggested that long term structural trends may substantially reduce the capacity of the rental sector in the future. (Emmanuel, p 30). If this turns out to be the case and if changing social and cultural systems affect the housing aspirations of young Greeks to any significant extent, then some of the policy responses developed in other European countries may have to be applied in Greece.

Portugal

The 10th Constitutional Government of Portugal contained, for the first time, a Secretary of State for the young and from 1985 onwards there has been a growing number of initiatives directed at young people. Young people themselves are represented on an advisory council set up by the new Secretary of State. While the bulk of the initiatives described below relate to the sphere of employment, there are also some which affect young people's housing opportunities.

Since 1986, and prompted no doubt by Portugal's membership of the European Community, employment initiatives for young people have flourished. For example, the Minister of Labour and Social Affairs introduced a scheme to improve the first-time job prospects of young people. Firms employing first-time entrants to the labour market do not have to pay the full contributions to the national social security and unemployment fund for a period of two years. Similarly, financial support is now given to young people aged between 18 and 25 who want to start their own businesses. The young recipients must spend at least 36 hours per week working for their new enterprise and the whole scheme is financed out of the European Social Fund.

In the sphere of education, initiatives have tended to focus on providing facilities for young people during the main summer vacation period. For example, the 'Open School' was developed for the children of immigrants and aimed to increase their knowledge of Portugese culture and hence assist in their social integration. The Schools were held in Braga, Braganca, Viana do Castelo, Vila Real and Viseu and catered for young people aged between 14 and 20 years. A slightly older group, between 16 and 25 years of age, participated in the 'Campo de trabaino' initiative which brought together young people from all over the country to participate in environmental and architectural preservation projects. In 1986 approximately 1,100 young people took part in this scheme.

A more ambitious scheme provided holiday jobs for over 35,000 young people in 1986. Operating during the months of July, August and September this scheme offers work for five hours per day on farms, in tourism, in some municipal departments and in research centres.

In relation to housing measures for young people the government has introduced two schemes to stimulate home ownership. The first consists of a general subsidy which declines gradually over the years and is available to all ages. The second is only available to young people, this means people under the age of 30 for individual applicants while for couples their combined ages must not come to more than 55 years. The subsidy remains the same for the first four years, then declines by one percentage point for each of the next two years and finally drops by two percentage points per annum thereafter. The only other measure that might help young people comes in the form of a loan available to people in rural areas of up to 15% of the value of their house if it is used for land acquisition. It is possible that land acquired in this way could be used to build a house for newly married sons or daughters.

Spain

The Spanish case study focused on Barcelona, essentially for pragmatic rather than theoretical reasons. While it is no more representative of the national situation in Spain than is the case in the other studies, Barcelona is interesting because it is currently accorded the status of being the youth culture capital of Europe. On a more formal level it is the capital city of the region of Catalonia and enjoys a relatively high degree of governmental autonomy via the Generalist (the regional government) and the Ajuntament (the municipality).

In the country as a whole there is growing recognition of the housing problems faced by young people, but public perceptions of the scale of the problems are slow to change. Nascimento (1988) suggests that this is because the family in Spain continues to play a strong mediating role between young people and their demand for housing and the state as a potential supplier. Moreover, 'the problem' is widely perceived to be one of the economic sphere, in particular young people's lack of access to secure, well paid jobs rather than one of the housing sphere, ie the lack of appropriate housing types. Within the economic sphere the most significant response at the national level to the problems faced by young people is the system of unemployment benefits. This operates on a contributory basis and requires the recipient to have worked for a certain minimum period. Young people who have short or non-existent work careers are therefore at a disadvantage. This has been recognised by the government which has raised the age of recognised dependency to 26 years. This has the effect of reducing young people's autonomy and shifting the burden of their support back on to the family.

Barcelona contains a relatively high proportion of young people, some 60% are under 45 years of age and 20% are aged between 15 and 24 years. The city has also received a large number of migrants over the years, although the vast majority have come from the rest of Spain rather than abroad. Of those from abroad, most come from Latin America and the rest of Europe and a minority come from North America (the Maghreb). This latter group is of most significance though as they constitute a visible minority and suffer from racial discrimination, along with gypsies and travellers.

In 1984 an Interministerial Commission published a report on the accommodation problems of the young and the creation of new homes. The municipality of Barcelona - the Adjuntament - responded to the report by making the following observations. First, that young people are prevented by the current economic crisis from becoming economically autonomous; second, that this is leading to forced overcrowding in many family homes, especially in areas of social housing and third, that these developments are stifling the young:

> There is a lack of housing for the new way of life of the young, their new and different way of understanding living and relating to one another, with alternative ways of living and working, not necessarily linked to the traditional urban and industrial culture.
> (Brozgo, 1985, quoted in Nascimento, p 14)

Policy proposals include a census of empty properties in the city centre, the rehabilitation of buildings in the older quarters of the city and an experiment to convert a public building into housing for young people. It has also been suggested that some of the housing built as part of the Olympic City in 1992 should be earmarked for young people.

Four initiatives are currently being undertaken by the municipality. The first is an information pack being prepared by the Youth Department which covers advice on house purchase, lettings and subsidies, legal advice and points concerning design. The second is a pilot project to rehabilitate a run down public building and convert it to eight units specifically for young people. The third is an initiative supported by the European Social Fund which is renovating 40 housing units in an old part of the city and the fourth consists of the development of a co-operative system to promote home ownership under the sponsorship of the Housing Department of the municipality.

Finally, it is worthwhile noting an initiative developed by the local authorities in Barcelona but inspired by the experience of a number of Italian cities. In 1985 the Projecte Jove was established to offer to the young people of Barcelona the opportunity to participate in the policy making process of the city. It worked on three levels; the commissioning of a study of the characteristics of young people in Barcelona; the establishment of consultation procedures and finally a dialogue with the city administration. While this initiative was based on participation and self determination there is evidence that some groups of young people, especially those most marginalised by society at large, rejected the scheme. Among the groups who rejected this initiative were 'the Heavies' who supported the musician Pedro Bruque, anarchists from the Ateneo Libertario de Sants and 'litroneros' more interested in beer drinking than in politics. (Nascimento, pp 17-20).

The initial study carried out by the Projecte Jove identified a number of areas for special action, including education, culture, sports and employment. Housing was not picked out in this way except to mention that the Housing Department was considering the introduction of measures to give young people greater access to housing. This reflects, yet again, the fact that in Barcelona and in Spain as a whole the problems that young people face when they try to leave home are not generally seen as housing problems. Moreover, it reflects an assumption that all young people are in a position to modify their aspirations for independent living as circumstances dictate. While this is often the case for the majority it ignores the problems faced by young people who cannot remain in their parents' home or do not have a home in which to remain.

CHAPTER 5: COMPARISONS, CONCLUSIONS AND RECOMMENDATIONS

This final chapter has four main aims. First, it rehearses the arguments for taking young people as the subjects of this research and for using an analysis of their accommodation situation as a lens through which the broader process of growing up and living independently can be studied. Second, it presents our main findings in a way that offers the basis for both a national and a local level of comparison. Third, it draws a number of conclusions about the likely position of young people in the 1990s and about the structures of opportunities available to them. Finally, it presents a set of recommendations directed at policy makers, practitioners and researchers at all levels throughout the European Community.

Background

The accommodation needs of young people are not to be set above the needs of others - the elderly, for example. Nevertheless young people are often regarded as crucial elements in the European population, and policies to ensure their integration into a future Europe lie at the heart of many of the activities of the Communities. The European Parliament and the Commission have often stressed the importance of young people as European citizens of tomorrow and have frequently expressed their concern at the gravity of the situation facing many young people. It is important to remember that, formally at least, most of the young people studied in the course of this research are already citizens of their respective nation states and, to some extent, of Europe. In 1985 the Commission issued a memorandum entitled 'Towards integrated youth policies in the European Communities' which identified a number of barriers to the active involvement of young people in decisions which affect their lives and suggested some principles for action. The barriers identified included lack of information about the range of opportunities available, the complexity and remoteness of many programmes available to young people and lack of effective demand from many groups of young people. The principles for action cover the acquisition of basic skills before entering the labour market; the establishment of clear contractual relationships between employers and young workers; greater equality of opportunity in local labour markets; the development of better links between employers and educational institutions; the encouragement of greater mobility; special support for the most disadvantaged groups of young people and finally, a respect for cultural diversity throughout Europe.

COMPARABLE UNEMPLOYMENT RATES
(UNDER 25 YEAR OLDS – AS AT NOV.88)

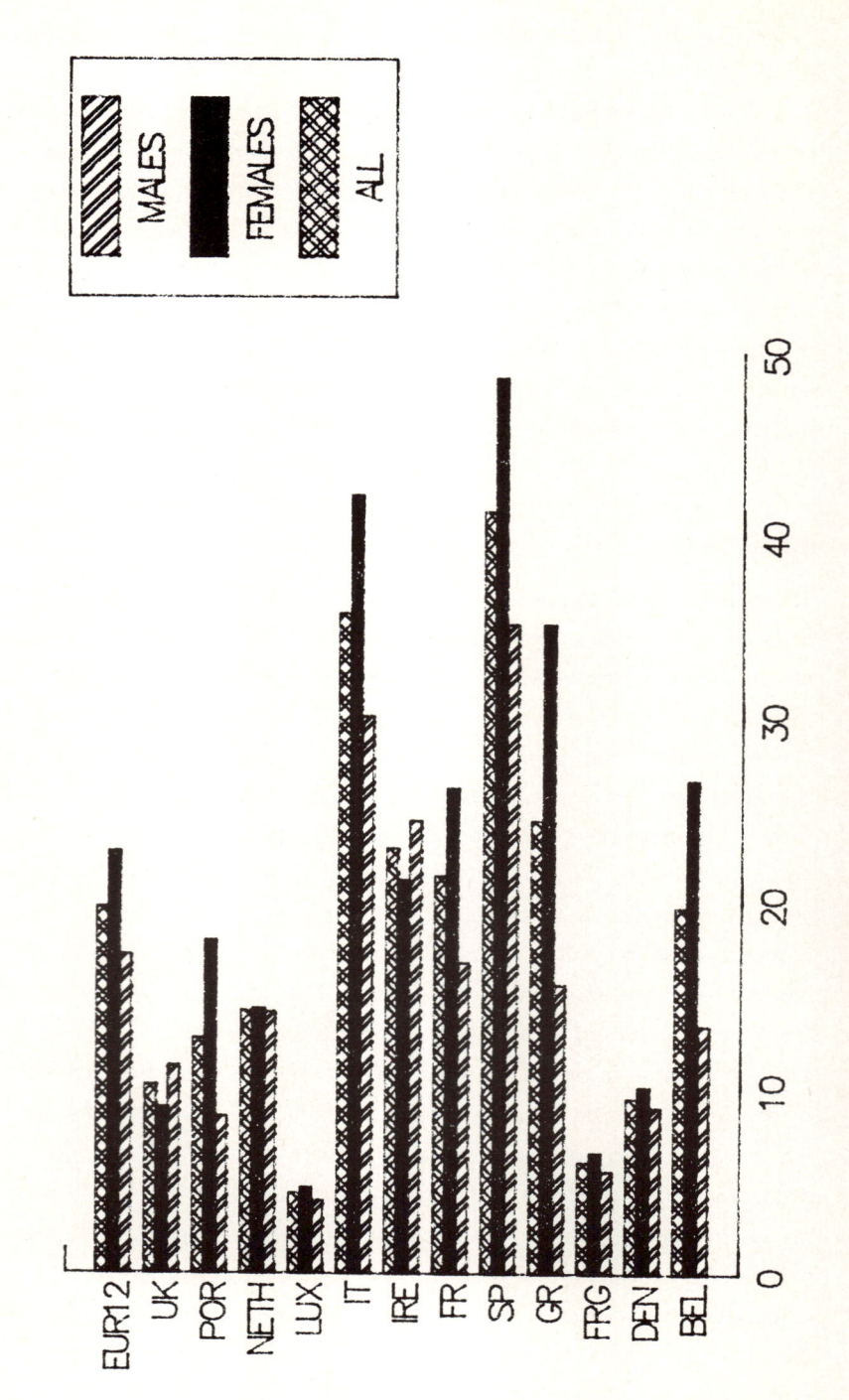

SOURCE : EUROSTAT – UNEMPLOYMENT 11/02.88

Notwithstanding these principles and the desire for greater policy integration, most European policy measures directed at young people have focused on only one aspect of transition - namely from full-time education to work. With high levels of youth unemployment (see Diagram A) attention has inevitably been given to prospects for work. Other aspects of transition, from living with one's parents to living independently or from youth to adulthood have not been studied in such depth or been the subject of such extensive policy development. The research described in this report reflects an important initiative by a Community institution to redress this imbalance. One of the main aims of the research was to look at some of the broader aspects of transition through the lens of young people's accommodation.

In this context the research has been informed by the extensive work undertaken by governmental and non-governmental organisations - many voluntary - which are concerned with young people's accommodation needs. The Foundation has been particularly conscious of the need to set the research within the broader context of related European policies and programmes. Homelessness, long term youth unemployment, the housing conditions of migrants and minorities, and participation in community development are themes of a variety of European programmes, not least the Programme of the European Communities to Combat Poverty. These themes are all echoed in this report.

In focusing on young people the Foundation was also very aware of the particular concerns being expressed across Europe, and indeed throughout the world, about the impact of homelessness on young people. Further direct assistance to the research came through the experience of the European Young Homelessness Group. The roots of this group lie in a conference held in Paris in 1980 to discuss a report produced by the French Ministere de la Sante et de la Securite Sociale. A network of delegates from other countries began to develop, including workers from France, Germany, the Netherlands, Italy, Belgium and the UK. Following the first conference in Paris further meetings were held in Strasbourg, Lille, Munster and Cork, culminating in a major symposium on 'Shut Out Youth' at the European Youth Centre in Strasbourg in 1987. In addition to acting as an international network the Group has also written about the wide ranging problems facing young people throughout the member states.

Since 1985 a series of motions for resolutions concerning homelessness and young people have been tabled by members of the European Parliament. In 1986 the Committee on Social Affairs and Employment decided to draw up a report on the topic. A motion for resolution was tabled in February 1987 and was debated in the European Parliament in June of that year when it was accepted without opposition by MEPs. The Commission however adopted a less positive approach and declined to accept any specific responsibility in this field or to devote any resources to the problems described in the report.

The report contained some 32 recommendations, proposals and other observations all of which relate to factors influencing housing opportunities in general. Some, however, are also specifically concerned with the situation of young people, for example:

> The European Parliament .... notes the particular problems faced by young people, and their housing needs and, taking into account the increasing numbers of young homeless people crossing Community frontiers in search of work and shelter, asks that special policies be framed in order to help them both within Member states and across national boundaries (for example, subsidization of cooperative community projects and of services within national schemes to help non-nationals who are homeless).

The recommendations described at the end of this chapter are intended to take forward this thinking and to contribute to the development of further policies which would widen the whole range of opportunities available to European young people.

Comparisons

At the _national_ level, comparisons between countries can be made on four dimensions:

- the position of young people in relation to the national labour market structure;
- the position of young people in relation to housing market structures;
- the form and role of families in different countries and the way in which they affect young people's housing opportunities;

- the attitude of national states to the wide range of problems faced by young people and to their participation in and integration into society.

The national case studies described in Chapter 4 above clearly demonstrate the disproportionate burden of unemployment borne by young people throughout Europe. This was especially the case until International Youth Year in 1985 when the Commission of the European Communities acknowledged that despite a range of measures undertaken at national and Community level the employment situation of young people had not improved. A new series of measures devised and implemented since then have begun to have an impact on the number of young people registered as unemployed. Along with an upturn in the economic fortunes of most member states the labour market position of young people in general has shown some signs of improvement.

<u>Although proportionately fewer young people are now registered as unemployed their spending power has not necessarily increased significantly.</u> Students in higher education and young people participating in the plethora of vocational training schemes do not usually receive an allowance comparable to a full wage. Without entering the debate about the appropriate level of educational grants or training allowances it is widely argued that these are often insufficient to allow young people to live independently, and have in some instances decreased in real terms.

On the second comparative dimension - housing - we can see the following points of similarity between different countries. Fiscal constraints have led to increased pressure on the social rented housing sector, although it must be remembered that this sector is not highly developed in some countries, eg Italy, Greece, Spain and Portugal. In the quasi-public sectors, that is autonomous agencies which receive forms of public support and subsidy, there is growing pressure to conform to commercial or profit-based market approaches in the distribution of the housing stock. This tends to act against the interests of the more disadvantaged groups, including young people at the start of their housing careers.

As the number of households continues to grow in most European countries so the pressure on this relatively static housing stock is growing. In some countries such as the UK the social rented stock is actually diminishing as council houses are sold to tenants and thereby transferred to the private sector. The result of this growing pressure is leading to tighter rules governing access to social rented housing and to stricter eligibility criteria. Measures to extend the private rented sector have yet to have any major impact on the totality of rented accommodation.

In many countries, but especially in the more prosperous northern European countries, national housing policies are geared to the promotion of home ownership. While this is often in line with the aspirations of many households it tends to vary with age and is usually less of a priority for young people. There is a <u>marked tendency for young people to favour rented property when they first leave home, mainly because it offers a relatively flexible and cheap form of housing</u>. However, in the face of redevelopment initiatives, the imposition of rent controls and long term returns on investment, the private sector has continued to decline in many countries.

The pace of this decline, the base from which it is taking place and the existence of policy measures which either inhibit or encourage further decline all vary by country, for example in the UK the decline began decades ago, in Greece it is likely to become a problem only in the future.

The third dimension concerns <u>the role of the family in affecting young people's opportunities for leaving home and living independently</u>. It is possible to detect two contrasting positions here which reflect to some extent the opposite ends of a continuum of western European experiences. At one end there are those countries where families play an enormously important role, in practice as well as ideologically, in terms of social control, social cohesion and, specifically, in relation to the transition of young people towards independent living. Greece, Spain, Portugal, Italy and, to a lesser extent, France all fit within this category. In these countries most young people do not expect to leave home and live independently unless they are getting married or entering higher education. Likewise there is very little evidence that young people would be forced to leave the parental home before they are ready to do so. While this sometimes leads to problems of overcrowding, it is suggested that young people benefit to the detriment of older members of the (extended) family.

At the other end of this analytical continuum are the countries where the role of the family has diminished in practice over the last decades even if its ideological significance remains high. In the UK, Germany, the Netherlands and France and Ireland to a lesser extent young people tend to want to leave home at slightly earlier ages and to do so for a variety of reasons and not just to get married. For example, the tradition of leaving home and living in shared accommodation with other young people is much stronger in the UK and the Netherlands than in Greece or Italy. It is probably highest in Denmark, a country we were unable to study in any depth (see, for example, Kiernan, 1986).

The final dimension refers to <u>political variations in nation state attitudes to young people in general and to responses to their housing problems in particular</u>. This dimension is obviously closely linked to the previous in that the family often acts as a buffer between the state and the individual young person, regulating demands for various services and being looked to as an alternative source of provision.

While many countries and indeed European institutions often refer to young people as an important resource for the future and develop measures to ensure their participation in public life, there is <u>little sign of young people constituting an effective political force as young people throughout Europe</u>. It is certainly the case that in some countries the demographic profile of the population means that young people form a potentially powerful voting bloc, Ireland, Spain and Portugal are the most obvious examples. It is unclear whether or not this can be said to lead directly to more or better state responses to the problems faced by young people, but it seems to provide a more favourable climate for youth policy development.

Within the research a number of specific <u>localities</u> were chosen for deeper study (see Map). These were picked to reflect two contrasting types of area - one of widespread economic decline and one of relative overall prosperity but with pockets of deprivation. The broad intention in selecting areas in this way was to enable a comparison of the housing opportunities available to young people in areas with very different job opportunities, and hence to examine the interaction of housing and labour markets and to allow an assessment of the overall socio-economic position of young people. We have also been able to consider, in a much more limited way, the situation in some capital cities.

CASE STUDY AREAS

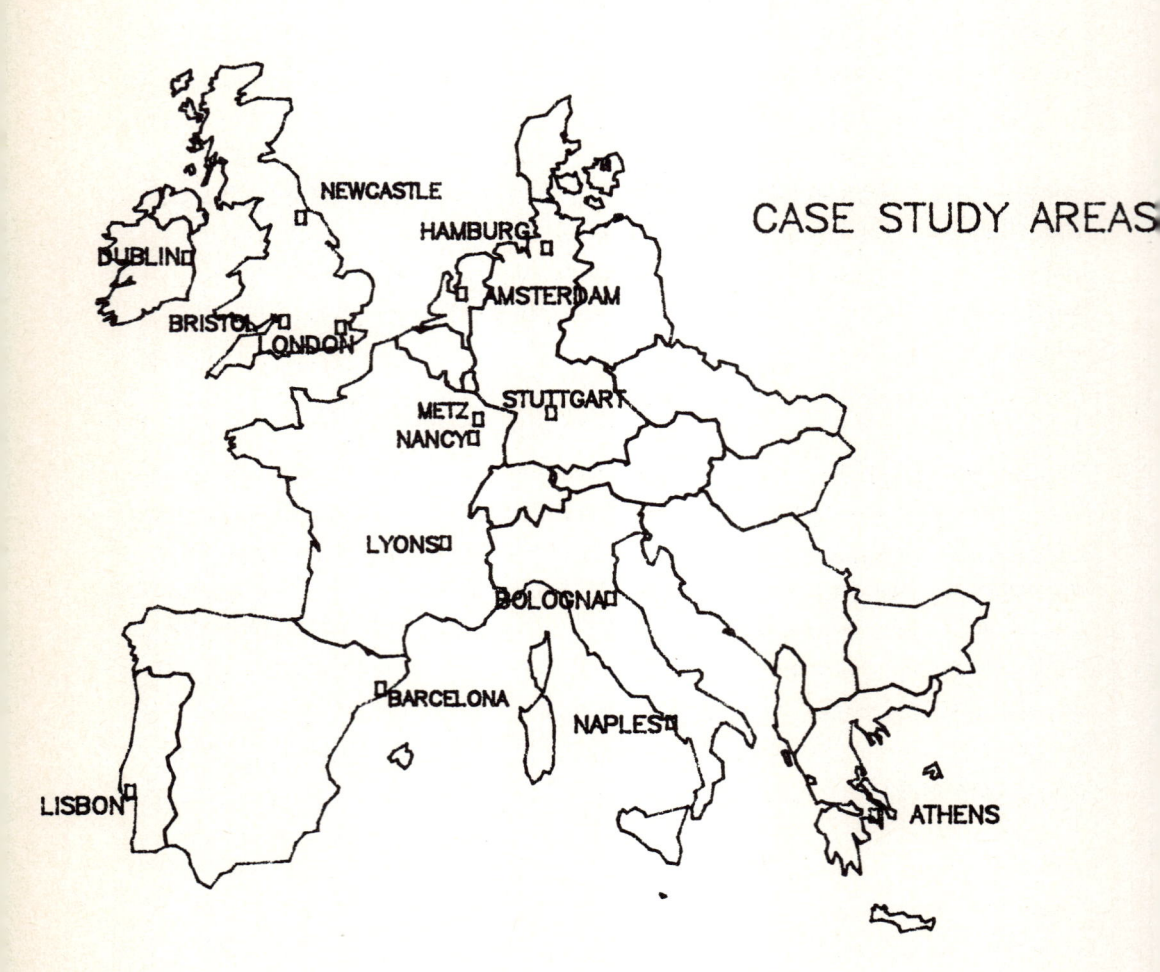

The areas of widespread economic decline include the north east region of the UK, Hamburg in Germany, Naples in Italy and Lorraine in France. In the Netherlands the Indian Quarter of Amsterdam represents an area of decline. The more prosperous areas chosen for study were the south west region of the UK, Stuttgart in Germany, Bologna in Italy and Lyon in France. The Ij and the Bijlmermeer in Amsterdam are described as 'emerging neighbourhoods' and are, or are in the process of becoming, relatively prosperous.

Within the <u>areas of decline</u> the following general similarities can be seen. There is often a relatively adequate supply of housing, including cheap housing to rent. Properties may not be in very good states of repair or be ideally suited to the needs of young and/or single people. Job opportunities are limited and tend to be concentrated in declining industries and those which rely on seasonal, temporary and unskilled labour. Wage levels are therefore low and this is often reflected in the volume of money circulating in local communities. Urban services tend to be poor, both in terms of quality and form of delivery and thus they do not tend to compensate for low levels of private provision.

In <u>areas of relative prosperity</u> there are, superficially at least, more resources with which to develop responses to the whole range of social problems including the housing problems faced by young people. However, we can see that in 'successful' cities such as Bologna, Lyon, Bristol and parts of Amsterdam, a propensity to redevelop older neighbourhoods is very strong. This is frequently associated with increased rent levels and house prices which act against the poorer sections of the communities which originally inhabited these areas. This tends to have a disproportionate effect on young people who are more likely to be poor and to live in these areas than most other age groups. In addition competition for scarce urban land results in high rents and prices throughout these cities.

We must, however, beware of placing too much emphasis on this typology as it is less applicable in some countries than in others. In the Federal Republic of Germany for example, while Stuttgart is generally more 'successful' than Hamburg some comparators do not conform with the typology. Housing costs are generally higher in Hamburg than in Stuttgart and the quality of urban service provision is also higher in Hamburg. Nationally agreed wage rates also tend to prevent the establishment of significant north-south wage differentials.

Young people are faced with a number of options in these cities - to spend a very high proportion of their income (from whatever source) on housing; to live in cheaper but highly unsatisfactory housing; to live in very overcrowded accommodation with a number of other (young) people or to move out of the city in search of cheaper accommodation, either commuting back to work or seeking work elsewhere as well. There is also evidence that some young people resort to highly dangerous strategies in order to get by and find somewhere to live, for example by turning to crimes including prostitution or by sleeping rough on the streets.

In the more prosperous cities housing markets tend to become highly segregated with pockets of extreme poverty existing close by areas of great wealth. Young people who are attempting to live independently for the first time are more likely to live in the poorer areas and <u>it is unlikely that their direct experience of the juxtaposition of extremes of wealth and poverty will encourage social cohesion</u>.

In relation to these two types of urban area, young people are faced with the prospect of remaining in an area where there are relatively poor job prospects, especially jobs that have long term security and good wage rates, but where access to housing is reasonable. The alternative is to leave the area in search of work but face the prospect of having nowhere to live in the short term or paying highly for poor quality accommodation.

While <u>capital cities</u> are usually relatively prosperous they often contain greater extremes of poverty and wealth than other cities. They have traditionally exercised a strong migratory pull both within their own country and abroad and this has a pronounced effect on young people who are among the most mobile sections of the population. It is often within capital cities that the gap between theory and practice or expectation and actuality is at its greatest for young people.

The most important conclusion concerning the <u>comparability and transferability</u> of the situation in different countries rests on the distinction between generality and specificity. Each of the national case study reports contains a wealth of details about the specific circumstances which structure young people's housing opportunities and the responses developed. Different institutional arrangements for providing housing, jobs, training, welfare and other forms of support hinder the transferability of some interesting local (and possibly national) initiatives. This is especially the case where local initiatives are geared to the exploitation of niches within these various institutional arrangements. For example, in England some very good supported hostel schemes have developed using money from the Urban Programme to fund capital costs of eg, conversion of buildings, and using workers funded under the Community Programme. Because these funding regimes are specific to England this aspect (the funding) cannot be transferred to other countries. The aspect that is most transferable is usually the underlying principle of the initiative and its general approach to working with young people. Hence we can say that schemes, projects, initiatives etc which involve young people in defining for themselves the problems they face and which then support them in devising solutions are among the most 'successful' in whatever country they happen to be.

Conclusions and prognosis

In this section we offer our conclusions on what are the most significant trends and processes affecting young people's opportunities and how these might develop into the 1990s. Before doing so we would like to stress that most young people manage the transition from dependent to independent living without experiencing any serious difficulties. This is especially the case when the circumstances of their leaving are seen as respectable or legitimate, for instance when leaving home to get married, to take up a job or further education or to carry out (often compulsory) military service. Under these circumstances resources are very often available from a range of support networks, including the family, local communities and the state. Young people who make the transition under less respectable or legitimate circumstances often receive less support. For example many young people run away from home and cannot therefore call on their parents for support or on statutory authorities which cannot by law offer them any assistance. Some young people do not have a family home to leave in the first place and arrangements for their accommodation - for example when they leave institutional care - are often inadequate. Young people in this position are frequently held to be personally responsible for the problems they face and responses are devised, inappropriately, on this basis.

It is important to recognise that the pressures generating greater mobility within the population of Europe will increase, and that in some respects the barriers to such mobility will be reduced. The essence of the single market in 1992 is that greater freedom of movement will be encouraged. Greater labour mobility will be one consequence and we are clear that whilst considerable attention is being given to the economic consequences of 1992 only recently has attention been directed to the social implications of a single market. The Commission itself has identified some 80 elements of work to be done on the social dimension of the internal market. Included within these social elements are topics relating to family cohesion and the freedom of families to move as a unit rather than a freedom confined solely to workers. This research confirms that recognition of the social aspects of economic integration are appropriate but that genuine mobility, and mobility of young people in particular, is dependent upon variables associated with urban living and accommodation conditions. If people are unable to find appropriate housing then labour mobility becomes a meaningless concept. This perspective emphasises the importance of accommodation to all the Social Partners and it should be emphasised that this report has direct relevance to employers and trades unions as well as the European Parliament and Commission and national governments. The Social Partners in different countries are already concerned in a variety of ways with the living conditions of young people through their contributions to finance for housing, through their support for the provision of advice on rights, and through their involvement with a range of community based initiatives as part of a broad social responsibility movement.

The evidence from different countries presented in this report and summarised below demonstrates <u>the centrality of housing as a factor in predicting the future living conditions likely to be experienced by young people in a post-1992 Europe</u>. We base our main findings and conclusions on this broad thesis and indeed restate it as we list these findings below.

Main findings:

1.   As Europe moves towards greater economic, political and social integration the need for flexibility in many spheres is increasing. In order to accommodate a (geographically) flexible European labour force there is a need inter alia for greater housing market flexibility.

2. There is, however, evidence which suggests greater rigidity. For example, policy measures to encourage home ownership tend to have this effect as do dwinding stocks of social housing. Private renting is becoming more expensive and the entry costs of both the rental and owner-occupied sectors are increasing. Cheap housing in many of the older inner city areas is disappearing in the face of urban renewal and gentrification. While in general there is more rationing applied to social housing, some areas are deteriorating so rapidly that they are sometimes let to 'non-priority groups' such as the young and single.

3. This lack of housing market flexibility is likely to have a particularly detrimental effect on young people. Having borne the brunt of unemployment during the last recession young people have, as a consequence, have been forced to surrender many of the labour market gains won in the boom years of post-war reconstruction. There are some signs, however, that in the medium-term future and demand for relatively youthful, skilled labour will increase and lead to an improvement in their relative position yet again. At the moment though it is possible to talk to a 'lost generation' who suffered from unemployment during the last recession but who are now too old to benefit from many of the policy measures targeted on young people.

4. There are signs in all the countries we studied of a small but growing minority of young people who are becoming totally excluded from the mainstream of society. There are many factors associated with these processes of exclusion and marginalisation, including the young person's class position, their gender and their ethnic or 'racial' origin. The extent to which young people have, or are deemed to have, serious personal problems also affects the likelihood of them being marginalised. Age in itself is not often a major direct cause of marginalisation and exclusion, although some age-based discrimination certainly does occur. Rather, young people tend to be more vulnerable to processes of discrimination and hence more susceptible to exclusion. The consequences of this type of exclusion for a Europe moving towards greater integration are profound. It is likely to prove very difficult to maintain or improve current levels of social cohesion if a significant group of people are systematically excluded from mainstream society.

5. Young people's exclusion is often inextricably bound up with their lack of access to proper accommodation. It is impossible to provide an accurate estimate of the number of young people who might be described as homeless or roofless, and even more difficult to estimate the number of young people living in inadequate or inappropriate accommodation. An indication of the magnitude of the problem can be gleaned from an estimate accepted by the European Parliament which suggested that 10% of the population of the Community could be classified as homeless. The European Young Homelessness Group has estimated that one million young people under 25 years of age are facing severe housing difficulties. While these estimates can be questioned, most agencies that have any dealings with young people or with housing problems report a marked incrase in the number of young people in various forms of housing stress.

6. Traditionally the family has acted as an important mediator between young people and major social institutions, such as housing and labour markets. Families often provide valuable resources for young people who are making the transition to independent living. This mediating role can, however, obscure the real level of demand or need for independent housing from young people and relieve pressure on both the state and the market. It is important to recognise this process as traditional family structures are being transformed quite dramatically in many countries. There is a real danger that social policies will be developed on the basis of out-dated assumptions about patterns of family formation and family capacities. It should be emphasised that we are not announcing the end of the family but proposing greater recognition of the diversity of forms that families now take. It is essential also to recognise that some young people do not have a family in the first place and may have been living in an institution until they reached the age of majority. Similarly, it is important to acknowledge the differential capacity of families to provide support for young people who want to leave home.

7. In a similar vein, local communities and neighbourhoods are often accorded an equivalent status to families when it comes to developing social policies. Again, while we accept the undoubted benefits of locally-determined actions and support locally-based initiatives, we would point out that many communities are starved of resources and are inexperienced in

developing their own capacities for self-help. This can often lead to local communities being given the responsibility for managing their own decline without any commensurate transfer of resources.

8. There is evidence that some young people are increasingly mobile and are travelling throughout their own countries and Europe in search of work and accommodation. Capital cities are particularly attractive in this respect. Some of the young people who suffer the worst housing conditions in these cities have arrived from elsewhere in the country or from other countries (not just member states). This may lead to some degree of transfer of individual and collective coping strategies -squatting of empty properties for example - which may in turn become the focus of conflict between young people and various state bodies. Despite moves towards greater integration it is likely that intolerance of alternative lifestyles will continue to have a detrimental effect on the lives of many young people who travel around Europe.

9. Responses to the range of problems faced by young people can be found at many levels, from national and international policy making bodies to autonomous, grass roots, self-help organisations. Many local level responses are excellent in themselves in providing emergency accommodation, advice, support or counselling for young people. Many groups campaign effectively as well.

10. The most appropriate initiatives are in the main those which respect the rights of the young people, which listen to their views and which enable young people to help themselves. The transferability of initiatives tends to lie in these elements rather than in the specific detail of what they do. Many locally-based initiatives survive and make a virtue out of exploiting niches in various systems - legal, welfare, housing, employment, financial and so on. These elements tend to be the least transferable within or between different countries.

11. Local initiatives are important but inevitably can only make a partial contribution. The opportunities available to young people to live independently in accommodation that is suited to their needs will not increase without the intervention of national and Community policy making bodies or a dramatic transformation in market provision. It is only at this level that macro-level processes which affect overall opportunity structures

can be influenced. There is a clear need for national and Community level responses which recognise that young people often face multiple difficulties.

12. Apart from those countries where young people constitute a significant political force *as* young people, there is little evidence of any willingness on behalf of policy making bodies to respond to the problems facing young people in ways which respect their rights to live as they choose. Again, the gap between the rhetoric of European citizenship and rights to appropriate service provision on the one hand and the reality of exclusion and insensitive provision on the other are unlikely to foster a sense of Community spirit among the young people of Europe.

13. As fiscal pressures grow and the resources available for social policy measures are more tightly controlled, so an increasing proportion of all responses to young people's housing difficulties take the form of emergency provision. While the need for this is undeniable it has a number of unfortunate consequences. First, it excludes all but the most desperate cases and may, on occasion, prompt some young people to resort to desperate measures to gain access to a service or facility. Second, it is reactive and cannot play any part in preventing young people reaching the stage where they need emergency provision. And third, it serves to stigmatise the process of growing up, leaving home and living independently when the opposite is needed.

Recommendations

This final section of the chapter presents a series of recommendations directed at policy makers, practitioners and researchers. We hope that we have not taken solutions that work in one national or local context and applied them indiscriminately to other settings.

The principles of local sensitivity and variation are recognised in policy development throughout Europe but we have not seen an equivalent degree of respect granted to young people as a specific age group with some specific needs in the spheres of housing and social policy. Our most general and widely applicable recommendation refers, therefore, to the <u>need to actively involve young people in all aspects of policy and practice which affect them</u>.

A second important principle must be the <u>recognition of the multiplicity of problems facing many young people</u> and the fact that they are frequently connected. Thus access to jobs is often conditional upon access to accommodation and vice versa and both are likely to be influenced by the young person's 'race', class and gender. This suggests that policies for housing, employment, social welfare, education, training and so on must be more integrated and attempt to have an impact on many different fronts at the same time.

This in turn implies that policy making bodies and institutions engaged in action for or with young people must be prepared to work in partnership with one another. Few organisations, even nation states or Community institutions, have the capacity to affect all the processes which influence young people's lives and so co-operation is necessary as well as desirable. Partnerships should also be encouraged between the different sectors - the public, the private and the voluntary.

Turning now to the main European institutions and to national, regional and local governments we offer the following recommendations:

> **We recommend that the Commission gives attention to the housing problems faced by the young people of Europe when setting priorities within action**

programmes and considering the distribution of Structural Funds. For example, the proposed Action Programme to assist the Long-Term Unemployed should take account of the housing needs of young people, especially the constraints on mobility imposed by rigid housing markets.

We recommend that national, regional and local governments recognise and acknowledge the range of problems faced by young people in search of appropriate accommodation and consider the impact of existing and proposed policies on the housing opportunities available to young people.

We recommend that all levels of government and indeed employers and trade union organisations reconsider any policies which directly or indirectly discriminate against young people on the grounds of their age.

We recommend that all levels of government encourage young people, and in particular groups of young people, to participate more both in the development of policies which affect their opportunities and in the development and management of initiatives such as co-operatives, self-help schemes etc. This will both foster greater social and political cohesion and develop more sensitive and appropriate policy measures.

In terms of good practice we offer the following recommendations, but would point out that it was never the intention of this report to provide detailed practical guidance to governments or organisations in each of the case study countries.

We recommend that support is given to the provision of emergency short-stay accommodation specifically for young people in all major towns and cities. This is essential to meet the immediate needs of young people who might otherwise resort to high risk strategies such as sleeping rough or engaging in street crimes in order to pay for somewhere to sleep. Some form of European network of such short-stay accommodation should be developed in order to facilitate mobility and ease the problem faced by mobile young people.

We recommend that short-stay accommodation is supplemented by facilities offering longer term residence. If this is not provided then emergency accommodation will become chronically over-subscribed and will be rationed in ways that do not reflect real housing need.

We recommend that both short and long stay facilities are supported in providing an integrated range of services. Many of the young people who use these facilities will have needs that can be met by specialists such as doctors, social workers and welfare rights advisors. At the same time it must be recognised that not all young people will have these needs or want to use these services and access to the facility should not be made conditional upon use of the services.

We recommend that young people are encouraged and supported in devising their own solutions to the housing problems they face. Housing co-operatives and self-build and conversion schemes have proved to be particularly effective in some countries and there is scope for their wider application.

We recommend that those organisations responsible either for housing provision or for advice give greater attention to providing information to young people about the services for which they are eligible and about the differing forms of accommodation which may be open to them.

Where young people are unable to participate effectively in local housing markets, consideration should be given to providing financial support in the form of rent subsidies, loans or guarantees, or otherwise easing the access of young people to finance for accommodation.

Local authorities should consider whether legal housing standards can be relaxed in order to facilitate new approaches to living, especially in old or redundant buildings. Similarly, regulations concerning the occupancy of vacant or derelict buildings may be revised to allow (young) people to meet their immediate housing needs. New approaches to design and rehabilitation should be encouraged to allow for more flexible responses to housing needs.

Finally, in relation to researchers and the funders of research we make the following recommendations:

We recommend that the Commission supports the establishment of a European network for all parties involved in the housing problems faced by young people, and that national governments do likewise in each member state.

Given our emphasis above on the active participation of young people, we recommend that research is encouraged and supported which draws directly on young people's own experiences and expertise. Research of this type is most likely to demonstrate the realities of the problems faced by young people to those who are in a position to contribute to their solution.

REFERENCES

Ball, M., Harloe, M., and Martens, M. (1988) Housing and Social Change in Europe and the USA. London: Routledge.

Bauer, G., and Cuzon, G. (1987) Urban Environment Housing Solidarity: Consequences for Young People: The French Case. Report for the European Foundation for the Improvement of Living and Working Conditions.

Burton, P., Forrest, R., and Stewart, M. (1986) Living Conditions in Urban Areas European Foundation for the Improvement of Living and Working Conditions: Dublin.

Burton, P., Forrest, R. and Stewart, M. (1987) Urban Environment, Accommodation, Social Cohesion - the implications for young people: English case study, European Foundation for the Improvement of Living and Working Conditions.

Deelstra, T. and Schokkenbroek, J. (1988) Housing for Young People in the Netherlands. Report for the European Foundation for the Improvement of Living and Working Conditions.

Di Palma, M., Pazienti, M. et al (1987) Urban Environment, Social Cohesion, Accommodation: The Implications for young people in Italy. Report for the European Foundation for the Improvement of Living and Working Conditions.

Emmanuel, D. (1987) Housing Problems of Young People in Urban Areas: The Case of Greece. Report for the European Foundation for the Improvement of Living and Working Conditions.

Focus Point (1987) Focus Point in Focus: Annual Report. Dublin.

Nascimento, George X. (1988) Housing and Living Conditions of Young People in Barcelona. Report for the European Foundation for the Improvement of Living and Working Conditions.

Jablonka, P., Potter, P. and Unterseher, L. (1987) Urban Environment, Accommodation and Social Cohesion: The Implications for Young People. Report for the European Foundation for the Improvement of Living and Working Conditions

Kiernan, K. (1986) Leaving home: a comparative analysis of six western European countries, mimeo.

Kroes, H., Ymkers, F. and Mulder, A. (1988) Between Owner-Occupation and Rented Sector Housing in Ten European Countries. NCIV, De Bilt, the Netherlands.

Mendes, C. (1987) The Housing Situation of Young People in Portugal. Report for the European Foundation for the Improvement of Living and Working Conditions

Ronayne, T. (1987) The Social and Economic Position of Young People in Ireland. Report for the European Foundation for the Improvement of Living and Working Conditions.

Other studies carried out and published by the Foundation in related areas:

Providing Information About Urban Services
(ISBN 92-825-7069-X)
(Also available in FR,DE,IT,DA,NL,GR,ES,PT)
Many people in high risk population groups do not know about services available to help them. This booklet is intended to encourage agencies to devote more resources to the development of effective ways of getting information to those who need it.

Living Conditions in Urban Europe
(ISBN 92-825-7054-1) — Information Booklet.
(Will be available in FR,DE,IT,DA,NL,GR,ES,PT early in 1990.)
An overview of current European policy relevant to urban living conditions, this booklet summarizes the impact of social and economic changes on the structure of cities and the quality of life in urban Europe. Trends in demography, family life, labour markets, housing provision and community involvement are examined and particular attention is paid to the processes of marginalisation which are creating and reinforcing social inequalities within cities.

Living Conditions in Urban Areas
(ISBN 92-825-6456-8)
(Also available in FR,DE,IT)
A wide-ranging review of research on housing and living conditions in urban areas, which examines trends in demography, family life, labour markets, housing provision and community development. The study also provides an overview of current European policy relevant to urban living conditions.

An investigation of activities for the unemployed: an annotated and selective bibliography
(EF/84/55/EN)
(Also available in FR)
The book is divided into three parts: employment situation and general policies; consequences of unemployment; and specific measures, schemes and initiatives for the unemployed.

Activities for the unemployed — Consolidated Report
(EF/85/67/EN)
(Also available in FR,DE,IT,DA,NL,GR)
Schemes which deal with the growth in the number of unemployed and the duration of unemployment have been developed in the Member States. They range from work-related projects to those providing social, cultural and leisure activities. Information has been collected on these projects in the various reports so as to assess their usefulness and to exchange information throughout the Community.

Activities for the unemployed — **Denmark** (EF/85/62/EN)
(Also available in DA)

Activities for the unemployed — **France** (EF/85/63EN)
(Also available in FR)

Activities for the unemployed — **Ireland** (EF/85/64EN)

Activities for the unemployed — **Netherlands** (EF/85/65/EN)
(Also available in NL)

Activities for the unemployed — **United Kingdom** (EF/85/66/EN)

Locally-based responses to long-term unemployment
(ISBN 92-825-8667-7)
(Also available in FR,DE,IT)
This report examines ways in which certain locally-based projects help the long-term unemployed to meet their needs, cope with their situation, and reintegrate economically and socially in the community. There are conclusions and recommendations to policy-makers and practitioners on ways to better combat long-term unemployment and to improve the living conditions of the long-term unemployed.

These and all other Foundation publications are available from the Official Sales Agents of the European Communities, the addresses of which are listed at the back of this publication.

The European Foundation for the Improvement of Living and Working Conditions

ACCOMMODATION AND SOCIAL COHESION IN THE URBAN ENVIRONMENT -
THE IMPLICATIONS FOR YOUNG PEOPLE

Luxembourg: Office for Official Publications of the European Communities

1989 - 107p. - 160 x 235 mm

EN

ISBN: 92-826-0020-3

Catalogue number: SY-56-89-287-EN-C

Price (excluding VAT) in Luxembourg:
ECU 12.50

Venta y suscripciones · Salg og abonnement · Verkauf und Abonnement · Πωλήσεις και συνδρομές
Sales and subscriptions · Vente et abonnements · Vendita e abbonamenti
Verkoop en abonnementen · Venda e assinaturas

BELGIQUE / BELGIE

Moniteur belge / Belgisch Staatsblad
42, Rue de Louvain / Leuvenseweg 42
1000 Bruxelles / 1000 Brussel
Tél. 512 00 26
CCP / Postrekening 000-2005502-27

Sous-dépôts / Agentschappen:

**Librairie européenne /
Europese Boekhandel**
Rue de la Loi 244 / Wetstraat 244
1040 Bruxelles / 1040 Brussel

Jean De Lannoy
Avenue du Roi 202 / Koningslaan 202
1060 Bruxelles / 1060 Brussel
Tél. (02) 538 5169
Télex 63220 UNBOOK B

CREDOC
Rue de la Montagne 34 / Bergstraat 34
Bte 11 / Bus 11
1000 Bruxelles / 1000 Brussel

DANMARK

J. H. Schultz Information A/S
EF-Publikationer
Ottiliavej 18
2500 Valby
Tlf. 01 44 23 00
Telefax: 01 44 15 12
Girokonto 6 00 08 86

BR DEUTSCHLAND

Bundesanzeiger Verlag
Breite Straße
Postfach 10 80 06
5000 Köln 1
Tel. (02 21) 20 29-0
Fernschreiber:
ANZEIGER BONN 8 882 595
Telefax: 20 29 278

GREECE

G.C. Eleftheroudakis SA
International Bookstore
4 Nikis Street
105 63 Athens
Tel.: 322 22 55
Telex: 219410 ELEF
Telefax: 3254 889

Sub-agent for Northern Greece:

Molho's Bookstore
The Business Bookshop
10 Tsimiski Street
Thessaloniki
Tel. 275 271
Telex 412885 LIMO

ESPAÑA

Boletín Oficial del Estado
Trafalgar 27
E-28010 Madrid
Tel. (91) 446 60 00

Mundi-Prensa Libros, S.A.
Castelló 37
E-28001 Madrid
Tel. (91) 431 33 99 (Libros)
     431 32 22 (Suscripciones)
     435 36 37 (Dirección)
Telex 49370-MPLI-E
Telefax: (91) 275 39 98

FRANCE

**Journal officiel
Service des publications
des Communautés européennes**
26, rue Desaix
75727 Paris Cedex 15
Tél. (1) 40 58 75 00
Télécopieur: (1) 4058 7574

IRELAND

Government Publications Sales Office
Sun Alliance House
Molesworth Street
Dublin 2
Tel. 71 03 09

or by post

Government Stationery Office
EEC Section
6th floor
Bishop Street
Dublin 8
Tel. 78 16 66

ITALIA

Licosa Spa
Via Benedetto Fortini, 120/10
Casella postale 552
50 125 Firenze
Tel. 64 54 15
Telefax: 64 12 57
Telex 570466 LICOSA I
CCP 343 509

Subagenti:

Libreria scientifica Lucio de Biasio -AEIOU
Via Meravigli, 16
20 123 Milano
Tel. 80 76 79

Herder Editrice e Libreria
Piazza Montecitorio, 117-120
00 186 Roma
Tel. 67 94 628/67 95 304

Libreria giuridica
Via 12 Ottobre, 172/R
16 121 Genova
Tel. 59 56 93

GRAND-DUCHÉ DE LUXEMBOURG

Abonnements seulement
Subscriptions only
Nur für Abonnements

Messageries Paul Kraus
11, rue Christophe Plantin
L-2339 Luxembourg
Tél. 48 21 31
Télex 2515
CCP 49242-63

NEDERLAND

SDU uitgeverij
Christoffel Plantijnstraat 2
Postbus 20014
2500 EA 's-Gravenhage
Tel. (070) 78 98 80 (bestellingen)
Telefax: (070) 476351

PORTUGAL

Imprensa Nacional
Casa da Moeda, E.P.
Rua D. Francisco Manuel de Melo, 5
1092 Lisboa Codex
Tel. 69 34 14

Distribuidora Livros Bertrand Lda.
Grupo Bertrand, SARL
Rua das Terras dos Vales, 4-A
Apart. 37
2700 Amadora Codex
Tel. 493 90 50 - 494 87 88
Telex 15798 BERDIS

UNITED KINGDOM

HMSO Books (PC 16)
HMSO Publications Centre
51 Nine Elms Lane
London SW8 5DR
Tel. (01) 873 9090
Fax: GP3 873 8463

Sub-agent:

Alan Armstrong Ltd
2 Arkwright Road
Reading, Berks RG2 0SQ
Tel. (0734) 75 17 71
Telex 849937 AAALTD G
Fax: (0734) 755164

OSTERREICH

Manz'sche Verlagsbuchhandlung
Kohlmarkt 16
1014 Wien
Tel. (0222) 533 17 81
Telex 11 25 00 BOX A
Telefax: (0222) 533 17 81 81

TURKIYE

Dünya süper veb ofset A.Ş.
Narlıbahçe Sokak No. 15
Cağaloğlu
Istanbul
Tel. 512 01 90
Telex: 23822 dsvo-tr.

UNITED STATES OF AMERICA

European Community Information Service
2100 M Street, NW
Suite 707
Washington, DC 20037
Tel. (202) 862 9500

CANADA

Renouf Publishing Co., Ltd
61 Sparks Street
Ottawa
Ontario K1P 5R1
Tel. Toll Free 1 (800) 267 4164
Ottawa Region (613) 238 8985-6
Telex 053-4936

JAPAN

Kinokuniya Company Ltd
17-7 Shinjuku 3-Chome
Shinjuku-ku
Tokyo 160-91
Tel. (03) 354 0131

Journal Department
PO Box 55 Chitose
Tokyo 156
Tel. (03) 439 0124

AUTRES PAYS
OTHER COUNTRIES
ANDERE LÄNDER

**Office des publications officielles
des Communautés européennes**
2, rue Mercier
L-2985 Luxembourg
Tél. 49 92 81
Télex PUBOF LU 1324 b
CC bancaire BIL 8-109/6003/700